Cambridge Elements

Elements in the Philosophy of Religion
edited by
Yujin Nagasawa
University of Birmingham

EASTERN PHILOSOPHY OF RELIGION

Victoria S. Harrison
University of Macau

CAMBRIDGE
UNIVERSITY PRESS

CAMBRIDGE
UNIVERSITY PRESS

Shaftesbury Road, Cambridge CB2 8EA, United Kingdom

One Liberty Plaza, 20th Floor, New York, NY 10006, USA

477 Williamstown Road, Port Melbourne, VIC 3207, Australia

314–321, 3rd Floor, Plot 3, Splendor Forum, Jasola District Centre, New Delhi – 110025, India

103 Penang Road, #05–06/07, Visioncrest Commercial, Singapore 238467

Cambridge University Press is part of Cambridge University Press & Assessment, a department of the University of Cambridge.

We share the University's mission to contribute to society through the pursuit of education, learning and research at the highest international levels of excellence.

www.cambridge.org
Information on this title: www.cambridge.org/9781108457484

DOI: 10.1017/9781108558211

First published 2022

A catalogue record for this publication is available from the British Library.

ISBN 978-1-108-45748-4 Paperback
ISSN 2399-5165 (online)
ISSN 2515-9763 (print)

Eastern Philosophy of Religion

Elements in the Philosophy of Religion

DOI: 10.1017/9781108558211
First published online: September 2022

Victoria S. Harrison
University of Macau

Author for correspondence: Victoria S. Harrison, vharrison@um.edu.mo

Abstract: This Element selectively examines a range of ideas and arguments drawn from the philosophical traditions of South and East Asia, focusing on those that are especially relevant to the philosophy of religion. The Element introduces key debates about the self and the nature of reality that unite the otherwise highly diverse philosophies of Indian and Chinese Buddhism, Hinduism, and Jainism. The emphasis of this Element is analytical rather than historical. Key issues are explained in a clear, precise, accessible manner, and with a view to their relevance to contemporary philosophical debates.

Keywords: Buddhist ontology, rebirth, Asian philosophy, emptiness, omniscience

ISBNs: 9781108457484 (PB), 9781108558211 (OC)
ISSNs: 2399-5165 (online), 2515-9763 (print)

Contents

1 Introduction 1

2 Self 6

3 Being and Emptiness 24

4 Nothing and Something 42

5 Pluralism 55

6 Global Philosophy 61

References 63

1 Introduction

This Element is unusual in its scope and range. The topic of Eastern philosophy of religion is potentially so expansive that the task of addressing it within a small Element such as this one could be compared to the task of doing the same with the topic of Western civilization! The reader should be warned that an attempt such as this can only be intrepid, and that what is presented here is the author's selective view on which philosophical ideas and debates have decisively shaped Asian spiritual traditions. As the reader will quickly notice, the most significant authorial choice was to emphasize Buddhist philosophy in its multiple forms as the thread that weaves together the otherwise very different Vedic and Sinitic thought worlds. This metaphor is apt because texts from all the traditions considered here are called sūtras, which literally means 'thread'.[1] The Vedic and Sinitic intellectual worlds were drawn progressively closer together by the continuous passing back and forth of important Buddhist sūtras. This explains the prominence of Buddhist philosophy in this Element relative to the other traditions covered.

By employing Buddhist thought, as it evolved first in India and then in China, as a pathway through a dense network of ideas, this Element introduces the major strands of Eastern philosophy of religion.[2] Philosophical systems, like Buddhism, that originated in the ancient world and matured over many centuries require careful articulation and introduction, for they are at home in thought-worlds that, in many fundamental respects, differ dramatically from our own. Despite the cultural and historical gap between the original contexts within which the philosophies considered in this Element developed and the probable cultural context of its readers, this Element will show that many of the key questions at the core of the philosophical traditions of Asia remain relevant to people today. This relevance is assured because these questions concern the self, the ultimate nature of reality, and the relation between the two: topics which typically interest reflective people from all times and cultures.

Readers of this Element should also be aware that the systems of thought introduced here are vastly complex and intertwined with continuously developing combinations of theory and practice. They also have important ethical, moral, and practical implications for the daily lives of those who actively practise the spiritual traditions to which the ideas discussed in this Element are intimately attached. Acknowledging this complexity, this Element seeks to

[1] 'Sūtras' is an anglicized pluralization of sūtra.

[2] This Element uses the terms 'India' and 'China' imprecisely as terms of convenience. The actual borders of both countries have expanded and contracted dramatically over the historical period covered by this Element.

elucidate the abstract philosophical assumptions and arguments that continue to inform living traditions of commitment and spiritual practice.

1.1 Outline

This section explains how the term 'Eastern Philosophy' is used and outlines what is included under the heading 'Eastern Philosophy of Religion'. It also briefly explains why the term 'religion' is problematic in the context of Asian traditions, suggesting that we need to broaden the typical Western understanding of religion if we are to appreciate the religious character of the philosophical debates that form the core of philosophy of religion in Asia.

Section 2 focuses on questions concerning the nature of the self within the early Sanskrit and Pāli intellectual traditions. Section 3 extends the debates introduced in Section 2 to cover broader issues, such as what it means to exist, and how being and non-being are related. Sections 2 and 3 are focused on Indian philosophy, although a discussion of Chinese Buddhism at the end of Section 3 leads into a focus on Chinese philosophy in Section 4. Section 5 introduces another important Indian philosophical tradition, Jainism, and explains why this tradition is especially relevant for the growing movement of global philosophy of religion that is the subject of the closing remarks in Section 6.

1.2 The Scope of Eastern Philosophy of Religion

The term 'Eastern Philosophy' can be used, somewhat imprecisely, to refer to the various philosophical traditions that developed in South and East Asia. These philosophical traditions fall into two main categories: those that emerged on the Indian subcontinent and those that developed on the other side of the Himalayas, in the region now known as China. The philosophical traditions of India and those of China are very different. They emerged independently, each drawing on a distinctive range of cultural resources and developing their own textual traditions (Halbfass 1988). Their trajectories of development only began to intersect with the transmission of Buddhism from India to China, which began just prior to the Common Era and picked up momentum over the following several centuries. Our knowledge of this early period of interaction between Indian Buddhism and Chinese thought is incomplete, and exciting new discoveries are still being made which sometimes change our understanding of this period. Nonetheless, we do know that Indian Buddhist philosophy took root in China and was transformed, under the influence of Daoist thought and practice, into the distinctive traditions of Chinese Buddhism. These new forms of Buddhism would later instigate dramatic developments within Confucian philosophy (see Section 4.12), but they had a more immediate impact on Buddhism in India. The meeting of Chinese and Indian Buddhism initiated a new and highly creative phase of Buddhist and Hindu philosophy in India (King 1997).

This complex history of the multiple transmissions of ideas across geographical barriers, times, and cultures – and the complex networks of influence involved – makes it difficult to reach a deep understanding of any one of the philosophical or religious traditions of Asia in isolation from an understanding of the others. This difficulty can itself become a barrier to readers approaching these traditions for the first time. One way to make this barrier less formidable is to focus on the subjects that interested philosophers in the ancient traditions of India and China. Many of these subjects are familiar to us today, such as ethics, logic, metaphysics, and philosophy of religion, although ancient philosophers did not make the sharp distinctions between these subject areas that many of us now take for granted.

Another characteristic of Eastern philosophies that can be confusing at first is that ancient thinkers did not distinguish the domains of philosophy and religion in the way modern thinkers tend to do. Nonetheless, looking back with our modern way of thinking in place, we can see that religious, or spiritual, questions and concerns were at the forefront of many of the early philosophical developments in Asia. For complex historical and cultural reasons, religious philosophy quickly assumed far greater prominence in India than it did in traditional Chinese, Japanese (De Bary et al. 2001), or Korean (Lee & De Bary 1997) thought. On the Indian subcontinent, philosophers were concerned with religious questions to a degree not found elsewhere in Asia. This explains why this Element focuses more on Indian than on Chinese philosophy.

1.3 What Do We Mean by Eastern Philosophy of Religion?

The term 'Eastern Philosophy of Religion' inevitably implies a contrast with its Western counterpart. Conceptually, this contrast makes sense, for Western philosophy of religion refers to philosophy concerned with Western religions (defined as Abrahamic religions), while Eastern philosophy of religion is philosophy targeted on the philosophical dimensions of the religions of Asia. In Section 1.5, however, we will see that the contrast between supposedly 'Western' and 'Eastern' philosophy of religion may be on the way to becoming obsolete.

There are many short introductions to Western philosophy of religion available. Most of these introductions canvas a predictable range of themes: the existence and nature of God, evil, faith, and so on. The contents of such books are predictable because the philosophical questions addressed are all generated from reflection on the central concept of Western theism: 'God'. By contrast, short introductions to Eastern philosophy of religion – in distinction to the broader subject of Eastern philosophy – are rare. This short Element may even be the first! One reason for this is that religions in Asia are generally not perceived to be sufficiently like one another to merit common treatment. They do not seem to be organized around a single shared central concept, in the way that Judaism, Christianity, and Islam are organized around the concept of God (even though in reality a cluster of concepts of God is at stake). In fact, it is increasingly acknowledged that the philosophical and religious traditions of India are more akin to those of the Far West (i.e., Europe) than they are to those of the Far East (McEvilley 2002). Consequently, an introduction to Eastern philosophy of religion cannot draw on an established range of themes, the discussion of which would serve as an effective introduction to the breadth of the philosophies of religion found in Asia.

In response to this problem, it is tempting to resort to presenting an introduction to the philosophy of religion in Hinduism, then in Buddhism, then in Daoism, and so on, through all the main traditions of India and China (and Japan and Korea). To do so, however, would inevitably result in a loss of philosophical depth in a short work such as this one. The alternative strategy, which I have chosen for this Element, is to focus on a small number of important topics, debate about which reveals the key trajectories of the evolution of philosophy of religion in India and China.

Section 2 begins the investigation of Eastern philosophy of religion by introducing a debate about the nature of the self. This debate began in India over two and a half thousand years ago and is still ongoing (Kuznetsova et al. 2012). The different positions that emerged within this debate came to define Buddhism in contrast to the Brahmanical tradition. The Brahmanical tradition was to become what people much later came to refer to as Hinduism (Flood 1996). This ancient debate about the nature of the self provided the impetus for the next key debate, considered in Sections 3 and 4, which concerned how to understand being and becoming. This second debate continued for many centuries, and it crossed back and forth between India and China. Rival positions were advanced by different schools of Buddhist philosophy in both regions. Non-Buddhist Chinese (Daoist) and Indian (Hindu) philosophers were also drawn into this debate, as eventually, as we will see in Section 4, were Confucian philosophers. Section 5 introduces a method of analysis first developed in ancient India by Jain philosophers. The method has been characterized as a form of epistemological pluralism, for it aims to show how apparently contradictory views – such as those advanced by other philosophers about the self – could, at least in principle, all be correct. Through exploration of this set of themes, this Element demonstrates that the religious philosophies of Asia, while not focused on a common concept, such as the concept of God, have several overlapping concerns. These concerns focus on understanding the relation between being and non-being (or 'emptiness', to use later Buddhist terminology) and on articulating the implications of how we think about this relation for our conception of becoming.

A concern with being, non-being, and becoming (or 'arising', as Buddhist terminology has it) is evident within Buddhist philosophy from its earliest appearance (Gowans 2003; Carpenter 2014). Indeed, it is no accident that Buddhist philosophy plays a central role in this introduction to Eastern philosophy of religion. Buddhist ideas and texts dealing with these issues crossed back and forth over many centuries across the trade routes which connected India and China. Consequently, the non-Buddhist philosophies and religions of India, such as Advaita Vedānta (King 1997), and those of China evolved in tandem with a Buddhism that was itself, as mentioned earlier, transformed by its encounter with Sinitic styles of thought (Liu 2006).

1.4 Problematizing 'Religion'

The meaning of the term 'religion' in the context of Asian traditions requires some clarification. Outside Asia, religion is often taken to have something to do with beliefs and practices directed towards God. This understanding is not too far off the mark with respect to the Abrahamic religions that are common in the West. However, this way of thinking about religion is too limited to cover religion in India and China. Buddhism is the obvious example of a religion that does not give a central role to supernatural beings, at least not in its earliest forms. The other two main traditions of China, namely, Daoism (Moeller 2004; Miller 2005) and Confucianism (Taylor 1990), also fall outside the standard Western understanding of religion. Nonetheless, adopting what has been termed a 'family resemblance approach' to religion, we can note that all the traditions mentioned in this paragraph share features that allow us to categorize them as religions (Harrison 2006). One such feature is the ubiquitous use of ritual along with the designation of specific places for its implementation, such as temples, shrines, churches, mosques, and monasteries. The traditions of Asia also share a concern for the spiritual or moral improvement of human beings, which is widely regarded as a core feature of religions.

1.5 The Future of Eastern and Western Philosophy of Religion

The philosophy of religion is now an academic subject with a global presence. One consequence, as noted in Section 6, is that the distinction between Eastern and Western philosophy of religion has begun to seem anachronistic to many people. Philosophers now often draw on ideas and arguments shaped by earlier philosophical work done both within and outside Asia (see Priest (2002) and Ganeri (2012), for example). Buddhist philosophy has become particularly well integrated into some ongoing philosophical debates (see Siderits (2004) and Garfield (2015), for instance). The sections of this Element introduce some of the most globally influential philosophies of Asia. The focus is on those aspects of Asian philosophical traditions that are of most relevance to religious thought and that are likely to be of interest to the new generation of philosophers of religion who work in an intercultural register (see Baldwin and McNabb (2019), for an example).

2 Self

The period between approximately 800 and 300 BCE saw a transition in religious and philosophical thought in the developing urban centres of the Indian subcontinent. The intellectual revolution that occurred during this period fed into the Sanskrit intellectual tradition in all its later forms. During this time, which is known as the Upaniṣadic period (see Section 2.3), several distinct philosophies became recognizable that were eventually to have an impact on human culture on a global scale. Buddhism was one such. At the core of early Buddhist philosophy, we find a set of arguments against an understanding of the self as non-material, unchanging, and eternal. (See Gowans (2003) and Siderits (2007) for detailed expositions of these arguments.) The eternalist account of the self that the early Buddhists rejected was widely held at the time by those in the Brahmanical tradition. Prior to the rise of Buddhism, it must have seemed to many a natural accompaniment to the widespread belief in rebirth.

In the Brahmanical worldview that Buddhism emerged in conversation with, the belief, which was later to become so important in the lands to the west of India, that there existed an omnipotent and benevolent God with consciousness and personality who cared about the fate of individual humans, was not to be found. Also absent was the belief that a God, or other supernatural being, judges individual humans and thus arbitrates over their post-mortem state. Without these beliefs, the spiritual life of people in early Brahmanical culture evolved in response to different concerns. Reflective people in the Brahmanical world forged an understanding of the spiritual significance of human life in relation to the universe as a whole. Their understanding was codified in the oral traditions that eventually became the texts of the four Vedas, which are the most important pre-Buddhist texts of the region and are still the foundational texts of Hinduism (Jamison & Brereton 2014). In addition to memorized oral traditions, ritual practices transmitted this received understanding and guided people through their current life towards a transition to their next rebirth. Spiritual life and religious practices were both premised on an understanding of the self and its connection to the whole (Ivanhoe et al. 2018). This explains why the questions asked about the self, and the various answers given, are not merely of anthropological or historical interest, but constitute the core of philosophy of religion in Indian traditions.

Philosophical debate about the self retained its importance within Indian philosophical traditions into the modern era. It became as central to philosophy of religion in India as arguments about the existence and nature of God did in the Western tradition. Over time, even within Buddhism, a plethora of rival views emerged, and the Brahmanical tradition itself gave rise to widely diverse perspectives. As we shall see in Section 5, Jains entered the debate with a rival theory, while also proposing a meta-theory that sought to integrate the many available views into a comprehensive understanding.

2.1 Outline

This section investigates a Buddhist view of the self as it developed in response to widely held beliefs in reincarnation. The section introduces what, for convenience, I will call the 'early Buddhist' position. The term 'early Buddhism' must be treated with caution though, for in the centuries after the death of the historical Buddha in approximately 405 BCE, many different forms of Buddhist philosophy emerged that all claimed to be based on his teachings (see Carpenter (2014) for an account of the main varieties of early Buddhist philosophy). Some of these forms of early Buddhist philosophy, moreover, had opposing views on central philosophical matters, such as whether impermanent objects were composed of micro-entities whose existence was permanent or not. This section presents the early Buddhist view in the form that became widely accepted in the later tradition of Indian Buddhism, the tradition that is now commonly, if anachronistically, known as that of Theravāda Buddhism (the Tradition of the Elders). In Section 3, other forms of Buddhist philosophy are introduced. These forms, which are collectively labelled as Mahāyāna Buddhism (Greater Vehicle), came to prominence in the Common Era and have been especially successful in China, Japan, and Korea (Williams 1989).

Section 2.2 explains the origins of Buddhism and related philosophical traditions, while Section 2.3 introduces the main texts to be discussed.

2.2 Origins

The details of Buddhism's origin during the post-Vedic, Upaniṣadic period (circa 800 BCE–300 BCE) are still contested, the main point of contention being the degree to which Buddhism emerged independent of influence from Vedic culture. Until fairly recently, most scholars assumed that Buddhism emerged from Vedic Brahmanical culture. This view has been challenged by Johannes Bronkhorst (2007), who has argued at length that Buddhism developed in the cultural region of Greater Magadha, which, although it was an Indo-Aryan region, was non-Vedic. Bronkhorst argues that Vedic cultural influence spread through Greater Magadha several centuries after Buddhism's emergence, and that this eventually led to Buddhism being perceived as emerging from the earlier Vedic tradition. Despite this uncertainty about its original context of emergence, it is clear that Buddhism did not develop in a context of cultural isolation but in conversation with the Vedic, Brahmanical tradition as well as with other schools of thought, such as Jainism, which were active intellectual forces at the time.

The origins of what we now call Hinduism are even more obscure. There is wide agreement that Hinduism is not actually a religious tradition at all, or at least that it is not a single tradition. 'Hinduism' is a term that covers a very diverse selection of ideas and practices that have been and are to be found on the Indian subcontinent and now also elsewhere. There is no single shared set of doctrines or practices that all Hindus adhere to or follow because Hinduism has always been constituted by a plethora of local traditions and lacks a centrally organized structure (Nicholson 2010). The main thing these diverse traditions have in common is that they are all shaped by ancient Vedic culture, although many also have roots in the even more ancient civilization of the Indus Valley, which flourished roughly between 2500 BCE and 1800 BCE.[3]

Introductions to Western philosophy of religion do not usually contain accounts of the origins of the religious traditions whose ideas are to be the subject of philosophical reflection. This Element largely follows this practice and refers the reader to several excellent introductions to early Buddhism (Gowans 2003; Harvey 2013) and to Hinduism (Flood 1996; Nicholson 2010).

The six philosophical schools associated with the Brahmanical Hindu traditions are distinguished as a group by their continued respect for the proto-Sanskrit texts of the early Indo-European Vedic religion (see Hamilton (2001) for a concise introduction to these schools). Buddhists and Jains reject these texts.

2.3 Texts

The key texts from the pre-Upaniṣadic Vedic period are the four Vedas (*veda* means knowledge in Sanskrit). The content of the Vedas was originally

[3] See the informative website: www.harappa.com.

transmitted orally but now constitutes a large body of proto-Sanskrit literature which very few people are familiar with in its totality. The most readable of the Vedas is the oldest, namely, the *Ṛg Veda* (see Jamison and Brereton (2014) for a recent English translation). Although few people read this text from cover to cover, some key passages are extremely well known, such as the hymn expressing a very ancient understanding of cosmic origins:

1. The nonexistent did not exist, nor did the existent exist at that time.

   There existed neither the airy space nor heaven beyond.
   What moved back and forth? From where and in whose protection? Did water exist, a deep breath?

2. Death did not exist nor deathlessness then. There existed no sign of night nor day.

   That One breathed without wind by its independent will. There existed nothing else beyond that.

3. Darkness existed, hidden by darkness, in the beginning. All this was a signless ocean.

   What existed as a thing coming into being, concealed by emptiness – that One was born by the power of heat.

4. Then, in the beginning, from thought there evolved desire, which existed as the primal semen.

   Searching in their hearts through inspired thought, poets found the connection of the existent in the nonexistent. (*Ṛg Veda* 10.129:1–4, in Jamison and Brereton (2014: 1608–9))

In the same chapter the *Ṛg Veda* contains other important verses (see chapter 10, verses 82 and 90) witnessing to the presence of theism in this early stratum of the Indian tradition. See Dasti (2012) for a survey and discussion of theism in Indian philosophical traditions.

The Upaniṣads were initially appendages to the four Vedas (Brereton 1990), which reveals the high regard in which they were held from early in their history (see Olivelle (2014) for an English translation of the oldest and most influential Upaniṣads). The Upaniṣads continue to be regarded by those in the Brahmanical tradition as sacred literature and have a place among the most widely read of the world's religious classics. Despite their popularity, the Upaniṣads can be confusing to read because they are not the work of a single author and do not present a systematic philosophical or religious view. Instead, they contain reflections collated over several centuries that question the meaning of the earlier tradition and, with their growing focus on subjectivity and self-knowledge, set a new direction for subsequent religious and philosophical reflection.

Later philosophical works in the Brahmanical Sanskrit intellectual tradition consist of texts developing germinal ideas found in the Vedas or in the Upaniṣads (Brereton 1990). These works – known as sūtras – each became foundational to one of the six main Brahmanical philosophical perspectives (*darśana*) that emerged following the Vedic period and were consolidated in the early centuries of the Common Era (many of these texts can be found in Radhakrishnan and Moore (1989)). The exception is the Sāṃkhya *darśana*. Their foundational text is the *Sāṃkhya Kārikā*, which reached its final form only in the fourth or fifth century CE. Based on each of these core texts, a long commentarial tradition evolved that formed the vehicle for original philosophical work (Ganeri 2001; Matilal 2002). This Element will not discuss all these philosophical perspectives and their texts (see King (1999) and Harrison (2019) for more comprehensive introductions). It will, instead, highlight just one: the tradition of Advaita Vedānta (see Section 3.9).

Buddhist and Jain philosophical traditions stood out from the Brahmanical mainstream during the Upaniṣadic period, because Buddhists and Jains did not accept the teaching of the early Vedic tradition, and hence were known as 'non-affirmers'. Each evolved an independent foundational textual tradition that set the agenda for future philosophical work. The early Buddhist texts are collected into the Pāli Canon (see Walshe (1995), Bodhi (2000), and Ñāṇamolí and Bodhi (2001) for English translations of the three key collections of early Buddhist texts). While the earliest Buddhist texts were written in Pāli, which is probably close to the language spoken by the historical Buddha, Buddhist philosophers in India soon switched to Sanskrit which was the common language used by scholars, much as Latin was in the West (Carpenter 2014: 242–3).

The texts mentioned here formed the bedrock of philosophical reflection on the Indian subcontinent. They were, however, the beginning and by no means the end of philosophy in this part of the world (King 1999). Philosophers and religious thinkers within the main traditions had a shared knowledge of these texts and freely referred to them as they went on to develop highly sophisticated philosophical systems over the extended time span between the end of the late Vedic period at around 300 BCE and the onset of modernity in the 1800s (Ganeri 2011, 2015a, 2017).

2.4 Rebirth

The philosophical perspectives mentioned so far in this section differed from each other in many important respects. Nonetheless, their philosophical disagreements were embedded in a context of shared understanding that included several key ideas. One of these key ideas was that humans and other beings are caught in a repetitive cycle of birth, death, and rebirth. This cycle of rebirth is known as *saṃsāra*. Escaping from *saṃsāra* can be regarded as the ultimate goal of the spiritual and philosophical traditions of the post-Vedic Indian world, at least until the Mahāyāna revolution of the early Common Era.

It can be difficult for people today to appreciate how compelling the idea of rebirth was to those in the ancient world. Many today unreflectively assume that time moves in one direction from the past to the future. Many also hold that this flow of time began with the origin of the universe and that it will cease when the universe comes to an end. These assumptions provide the context in which a human life is envisaged as directed like an arrow, passing through time in one direction, with a definitive beginning and a definitive end. Such a conception of human life would, however, have been very unusual to find within the thought-world of early Indian philosophy of religion. Within the culture of early India, as in all early cultures, time was thought to move in cycles. Consider how one cycle of the sun is followed by another, and another, and another. The cyclical understanding of time is closely related to the way people must have experienced the natural world in pre-modernity, with its agricultural cycles, the lunar and solar cycles, and so on. This experience of predictable repetition in the natural world provides the context for a view of biological life that sees human beings as the subjects of cyclical repetition. A human life cycle was envisaged as similar to that of a plant that slowly grew, bore fruit and seeds, before disintegrating in its current form, only to reappear in another embodiment when the seeds sprouted. There are many variations within different views of rebirth, although the essence of all of them is the belief that a person's death is not the end for them as they will be reborn into another form (Burley 2016). The transition from one embodiment to the next that was thought to follow death was generally regarded to be without a natural end.

A well-known passage in the *Bṛhadāraṇyaka Upaniṣad* reads:

> A man who's attached goes with his action,
> to that very place to which
> his mind and character cling.
> Reaching the end of his action,
> of whatever he has done in this world –
> From that world he returns
> back to this world,
> back to action.
>
> (*Bṛhadāraṇyaka Upaniṣad* 4.4.6, Olivelle's (2014: 121) translation)

Although there is little evidence that belief in rebirth was held within earlier Vedic culture, it became so widely accepted from the Upaniṣadic period onwards that no attempts can be found in early Indian texts to defend it as a philosophical idea. This absence of argument makes sense considering that there is no need to provide arguments for beliefs that virtually everyone holds. Only when a view runs contrary to what people generally believe are philosophers roused to mount defences and proffer justification for holding or rejecting the view. No philosopher today, for example, is concerned to provide an argument justifying the widely held belief that people die. This consideration partly explains the lack of arguments defending belief in rebirth in the early Indian material.

To ask today how philosophers in early India attempted to justify belief in rebirth would be to ask the wrong question. As Mikel Burley has argued, we can do better by trying to understand the significance of the idea of rebirth (Burley 2016). In the next section, we begin by considering whether it was regarded as a good thing or a bad thing for a human to be reborn.

2.5 Is Rebirth Good or Bad?

Many people today, especially younger people from relatively affluent families, find the idea of rebirth highly attractive. They are dissatisfied with the thought that this one life might be the only one they will have, and the prospect of an endless series of lives – all as enjoyable as their current one – seems vastly preferable to a definitive end in death.[4] This perspective, however, is not to be found in early Indian philosophy, and it can present an obstacle to understanding the meaning and significance of rebirth within pre-modern Indian thought.

The idea that the ultimate spiritual goal is to be released from *saṃsāra* (the cycle of rebirth) is held by Hindus, Buddhists, and Jains. All of them, in one way or another, hold that rebirth into another physical form is a bad thing insofar as it commits us to another lifetime in the realm of causation, confusion, and suffering. Rebirth is also the ticket to another death, before the occurrence of which we are likely to suffer greatly because of natural and seemingly unavoidable changes within the human life cycle, such as the transition from maturity to old age. We are also likely to suffer when we experience the death of those we love.

The perspective just described is not as alien to modern human experience as it might initially have seemed. Many of us will be familiar with the intense suffering that occurs when someone close to us dies. We can perhaps imagine that we have already experienced this suffering repeatedly in a vast number of

[4] These remarks are based on the author's experience of discussing these issues in university classrooms over multiple decades and in the United States, the United Kingdom, and Macao.

previous lifetimes, and that we will continue to experience it in a potentially infinite number of future lifetimes. This thought experiment can yield a visceral sense of the horror with which rebirth was regarded in post-Upaniṣadic culture. It can also shed light on why many felt it to be so urgent to escape from this deadly cycle.

The passage from the *Bṛhadāraṇyaka Upaniṣad* quoted in Section 2.4 goes on to provide advice about how one might break out of the deadly cycle of rebirth:

> Now, a man who does not desire – who is without desires, who is freed from desires, whose desires are fulfilled, whose only desire is his self – his vital functions (*prāṇa*) do not depart. *Brahman* he is, and to *brahman* he goes. (*Bṛhadaraṇyaka Upaniṣad* 4.4.6, in Radhakrishnan and Moore (1989: 87))

Having established that, in the post-Upaniṣadic period, rebirth is widely regarded not only as a bad thing for a person but also as the worst thing that can happen, as it exposes the person to a potentially infinite amount of suffering, we can turn to the question of 'Who or what is the subject of rebirth?' A very early stratum of philosophical debate in India developed around different attempts to answer this question. Brahmanical and Buddhist schools of philosophy came to be defined by the answers they gave.

2.6 Who or What Is Reborn?

Rebirth is a complex topic, and it would be impossible to do justice to it in the short space available here. The reader should, therefore, be warned that what follows is a simplification (see Burley (2016) for a more comprehensive discussion).

At first glance, the idea of rebirth seems to presuppose that a person can survive the death of their physical body. Although this idea is not found in the early Vedic tradition, it is present in the Upaniṣads (see Sections 2.4 and 2.5). In what shall be referred to here in general terms as 'the Brahmanical view', the part of a person that was thought to pass from one physical body to another in the process of birth, death, and rebirth was known as the *ātman* (*ātman* is the Sanskrit word, in Pāli the word used is *attā*). While it might be initially tempting to interpret this term as referring to the psychological dimension of a person, encompassing their character, personality, and memories, this would not capture the meaning of the Sanskrit term. Such an interpretation would be inadequate because *ātman* was not held to be constituted by the psychological dimension of a person at all. If a deceased person's character, personality, or memories do seem to leave some imprint on a subsequent embodiment, it would be an accidental feature of the new embodiment not an essential one (perhaps the result of a traumatic death).[5] The teaching of the Upaniṣads is that *ātman* is unchanging and everlasting and that it is one with the ultimate reality of the cosmos, known as *Brahman* (see Section 2.5). Properly speaking, then, on this view, *ātman* has neither physical nor psychological properties.

The view that became widespread in the Brahmanical tradition was that each human embodiment is somehow related to an unchanging and everlasting *ātman*. Being unchanging and everlasting means that the *ātman* can neither die nor be reborn because death and rebirth require change. All individual human lives came to be understood in relation to this eternalist context. The central problem set for post-Vedic philosophy of religion was how to give an account of the relation between the phenomenology of a human life as it is experienced and a postulated unchanging, everlasting *ātman*, which was thought to be entirely transcendent to that experience. If the true self is the *ātman*, then the self that each of us is aware of subjectively and individually (and that we each identify as 'I') cannot be who or what we really are. If this view is correct, at a very fundamental level, most humans are radically mistaken about their own identity. This explains why many ancient Indian philosophical systems regard the core problem confronting human beings as ignorance about the true nature of the self. A secondary problem for post-Vedic philosophers, which follows from the first, was how to explain continuity between different embodied human lives. In virtue of what might we say that one person is the reborn form of an earlier one? Both these problems concern the struggle to articulate what the identity of a self can mean, considering the tension between continuity and change. We can note that this is the same basic issue that continues to vex philosophers today who focus on problems of personal identity and selfhood, for the tension between continuity and change is found in all human lives that last long enough. We do not have to bring rebirth into the picture to see what the philosophical problem is.

Karma, like rebirth, is an idea that forms part of the shared cultural understanding that shaped the post-Vedic traditions. It has been speculated that the idea of *karma* came into early Indian thought as an attempt to explain the continuity between different embodied human lives (McEvilley 2002). The view developed that *karma* was a form of non-physical causation that linked one embodied life to another. While this basic view of *karma* was widely shared

5 Nonetheless, it should be acknowledged that common to many conceptions of rebirth, both ancient and modern, is the idea that character traits can be transferred from one life to the next. It is also commonly held that, given a sufficient level of spiritual attainment, it is possible to recall one's previous lives. The account of the Buddha's awakening contains the claim to have recalled 'a hundred thousand' previous lives. (See *Saṃyutta Nikāya* II: 213–14, in Bodhi (2000: 673–4).) For a discussion of some of the philosophical issues arising from claims to remember past live, see Burley (2016: chapter 2).

(except by the Jains, who held *karma* to be physical), many different views developed purporting to explain the mechanism of *karma*. One of the most influential of these views is found in early Buddhist thought.

Siddhārtha Gautama (Siddhattha Gotama, in Pāli) lived between approximately 485 and 405 BCE. After his experience of awakening (which is discussed in Sections 2.7 and 2.8), he became known as the Buddha, the Awakened One. The title 'Buddha' came from the Pāli word *bodhi*, which means 'awakened intellect'. Much has been written about Siddhārtha Gautama's life, both before and after he became known as the Buddha, and there are many legends about him (Schmidt-Leukel 2006: 19–29). Siddhārtha laid the foundations for a new approach to understanding human persons that attempted to break free of the cluster of problems outlined above. He rejected the claim that what ties together a series of rebirths is their connection to an unchanging, eternal *ātman* that was permanently fixed in an inaccessible realm transcendent to our experience. This new approach did not directly refute the claim that there was an unchanging *ātman*, as the Brahmanical tradition held. Instead, the Buddha proposed an alternative account of human persons, rebirth, *karma*, and liberation (Gowans 2003; Siderits 2004) that claimed to be closer to actual experience than the Brahmanical one. In so doing he revolutionized the framework within which many people thought about issues concerning human persons, rebirth, *karma*, and liberation. The Buddha and his many disciples believed this new framework to be more effective than the former one in helping people to achieve liberation from rebirth and suffering.

2.7 Liberation

The foundations of the early Buddhist understanding of persons are found in the following passage (and in many other early Buddhist texts from the Pāli Canon):

> I could see as it really is the primary characteristic of human existence [i.e., suffering], how it arises, that it can cease, and the way leading to its cessation. I knew as they really are the continuity tendencies, their arising, their ceasing, and how to achieve their cessation. Knowing and seeing thus, my mind achieved freedom from the binding effects of holding to opinionated views, and my mind achieved freedom from the binding effects of ignorance. I then knew for certain that I was liberated from rebirth, I had practised what was necessary, done what had to be done, and my present state would generate no further continuity. (*Vinaya* III.4. paraphrased in Hamilton (2001: 45))

Most scholars take this first-person narrative to be directly derived from the Buddha's oral teaching, which was based on the insights he gained during his own experience of awakening. The narrative combines an analysis of human experience with an account of how to achieve liberation by avoiding rebirth. The English word 'liberation' is a translation of the Sanskrit term *nirvāṇa* (which literally means 'extinction', the Pāli term is *nibbāna*).[6] The Buddha taught that *nirvāṇa* occurs when the cycle of rebirth is broken. He distinguished between *nirvāṇa*-in-this-life, the state of one who is still living but has awakened, and final *nirvāṇa* (known as *paranirvāṇa*), which is reached when the awakened one dies. The narrative makes clear that the cessation of suffering is closely connected to the state of being liberated from rebirth, for when one is liberated from rebirth one's suffering will have ceased (see Section 2.15 on cessation).

The passage quoted above also emphasizes the role of knowledge in liberation, thus permanently establishing philosophy as an essential component of Buddhist practice. Within all later forms of Buddhism, philosophy retained a central place alongside meditation, which was another practice established by the Buddha (although it was not the exclusive preserve of Buddhists, being already well established in Indic culture by the time of the Buddha). Despite many other developments, philosophy has remained tied to meditation within Buddhism and has never become detached from its original soteriological purpose (Shulman 2014).

Ultimately, Buddhism established a three-pronged approach to arriving at liberation. This approach blended wisdom, ethical commitment to a lifestyle structured by the idea of avoiding harm to others and to oneself, and meditation (Vetter 1988). This approach is schematized in the well-known eightfold path, which provides the framework for life as a Buddhist:

Right Understanding
Right Intention
Right Speech
Right Action
Right Livelihood
Right Effort
Right Mindfulness
Right Concentration

Traditionally, the elements of the eightfold path are distributed between wisdom (*prajñā* in Sanskrit, *pañña* in Pāli), ethics (*śīla* in Sanskrit, *sīla* in Pāli), and meditation (*samādhi* in both Sanskrit and Pāli) in this way: right understanding (sometimes translated as 'right view') and right intention contribute to wisdom; right speech, right action, and right livelihood are components of an ethical life

[6] For the sake of clarity, throughout this Element, I give both the Sanskrit and Pāli terms when discussing concepts important to early Buddhism. When discussing later developments within Mahāyāna traditions, I provide Sanskrit and Chinese terms where they are relevant.

(Harvey 2000); right effort, right mindfulness, and right concentration concern meditation (Takeuchi 1997).

The Buddha taught that a life shaped by the eight precepts of the Buddhist path would be a life in the process of radical transformation. A core part of this transformation would be intellectual, for the first precept, right understanding, refers specifically to an understanding of the Buddha's teaching. This teaching is encapsulated in the four noble truths.

2.8 The Four Noble Truths

The four noble truths can be regarded as the four key insights gained by the Buddha during his awakening. They are the bedrock of Buddhist teaching and can be found in slightly different formulations in many early Buddhist texts (including the passage discussed in Section 2.7).

The first insight is that suffering (*duḥkha* in Sanskrit, *dukkha* in Pāli) is a pervasive feature of human experience.

> Now this ... is the noble truth of suffering: birth is suffering, aging is suffering, illness is suffering, death is suffering; union with what is displeasing is suffering; separation from what is pleasing is suffering; not to get what one wants is suffering; in brief, the five aggregates subject to clinging are suffering. (*Saṃyutta Nikāya* 56:11, in Bodhi (2000: 1844))

The second insight concerns the origin or cause of suffering.

> Now this ... is the noble truth of the origin of suffering: It is this craving [*tṛṣṇā* in Sanskrit, *tanhā* in Pāli] which leads to renewed existence, accompanied by delight and lust, seeking delight here and there; that is, craving for sensual pleasures, craving for existence, craving for extermination. (*Saṃyutta Nikāya* 56:11, in Bodhi (2000: 1844))

The second insight leads to the third, which is the realization that suffering can cease.

> Now this ... is the noble truth of the cessation of suffering: It is the remainderless fading away and cessation of that same craving, the giving up and relinquishing of it, freedom from it, nonreliance on it. (*Saṃyutta Nikāya* 56:11, in Bodhi (2000: 1844))

Finally, the third insight leads to the fourth, which concerns how to bring about an end to suffering.

> Now this ... is the noble truth of the way leading to the cessation of suffering: It is this Noble Eightfold Path; that is, right view, right intention, right speech, right action, right livelihood, right effort, right mindfulness, right concentration. (*Saṃyutta Nikāya* 56:11, in Bodhi (2000: 1844))

This is neither the place to give a full account of Buddhist philosophy nor to elaborate on the complexity of meaning carried by the word (*duḥkha / dukkha*) that is here being translated into English as suffering. Instead, Sections 2.9 to 2.14 focus on explaining those aspects of the Buddha's teaching that particularly concern his understanding of human persons and their subjective experience. Gaining right understanding (or right view) of these matters is regarded by Buddhists, and others in the post-Vedic Indian traditions, as being of great spiritual importance. As will be explained in Section 2.9, the idea of impermanence lies at the heart of the Buddhist understanding of persons. Despite the substantial variations between different styles of Buddhist philosophy that began to develop after the Buddha's death from the starting point of the teaching schematized in the four noble truths and the eightfold path, the basic teaching on impermanence (*anitya* in Sanskrit, *anicca* in Pāli) was accepted by all Buddhists and so can safely be regarded as one of the core teachings of Buddhism.

As we have seen, the Buddha provided answers to two questions: 'What causes the human experience of suffering?' and 'What causes rebirth?' The answers to both questions turned out to be closely connected. Impermanence causes human suffering because of the attachments we form to transitory things, and attachment to these things then fuels rebirth. The Buddha's key insight was that understanding of this deadly dynamic could be gained by looking very closely at the causal relationships running between the impermanent psychological and physical realities that we experience and the effects that these have on us. This insight led to the distinctive Buddhist analysis of the phenomenology of experience that supports the early Buddhist understanding of persons.

2.9 Impermanence

The Buddha's analysis of human experience and subjectivity is premised on the realization that all our experience is transitory. The intuitive force of this realization is easy for most people to grasp; indeed, it may be difficult to avoid. It is obviously true that our hedonic experiences of pleasure and pain are transitory. Consider that even the most pleasurable experience will give way to discomfort and then to pain if it continues for long enough. The first glass of a chocolate milkshake might be delicious, the next two less so. If one continues to drink, one's experience will transition quickly into discomfort and then pain. Perceptual experience is also transitory. Sounds, odours, and colours come and go as we move our heads and otherwise re-position our bodies in space. Whether or not we ourselves are moving, we might notice that our perceptions also change, and sometimes quite rapidly, with the passage of time.

Reflection reveals that not only is our experience transitory, the objects of that experience are also impermanent. Artefacts easily break and disintegrate, while natural objects have a variety of lifespans. Some trees, for example, have a natural lifespan of only a few years, while a Giant Sequoia can live for over 4,000. Most of the physical objects we encounter in our day-to-day lives exist for relatively short periods of time. It is telling that few people have many objects in their personal possession that are over, say, 150 years old (and most of their possessions probably only last a few years).

As even quite young children can realize, impermanence is also a characteristic of human beings. People change from birth, through childhood, adulthood, and finally through the process of dying. After a certain point in life, most people become painfully aware of the changes they undergo through time, as well as those undergone by others. Birth and death are probably the most dramatic changes, but even these are part of a continuum. Human relationships are also vulnerable to impermanence. Parents and children, husbands, wives and partners, even beloved canine friends can be injured and will eventually die.

The upshot is that there is nothing either within our subjective experience or within the range of physical objects we might encounter in the world that does not change (sadly, as we have seen, this includes our own bodies). Everything is impermanent. Failing to understand this, and especially failing to realize that it also applies to ourselves, in the Buddha's analysis, condemn us to future rebirth. This is because if we fail to understand that everything is impermanent, we will continue to crave things that inevitably pass out of our grasp. While understanding of impermanence is necessary for liberation, it is not, however, sufficient. The Buddha taught that to achieve liberation from rebirth acceptance of impermanence is also required.

The Buddha realized that one of the most powerful psychological barriers to acceptance of his teaching about impermanence was the attachment many people in his era felt to the idea of themselves as being constituted by a permanent, unchanging *ātman* (*attā* in Pāli) (see Section 2.6). The *ātman* of the Brahmanical tradition was a perfect object for attachment, as it was conceived to be a self that was transcendent to the trials and indignities of life. Because of the perceived danger of this idea, early Buddhist philosophers sought to replace it with what they took to be a more accurate account of human persons. They first argued, rather plausibly, that nothing within our experience gives us any reason to think that we have within us a permanent, unchanging, eternal self (see Section 2.10). This conclusion was then employed as the basis for an account of human persons that rivalled the Brahmanical one by more effectively explaining the phenomenology of our experience.

2.10 The Five Bundles

The early Buddhist account of human persons is a philosophical extrapolation of the experiences the Buddha had during meditation, and it can be regarded as based on an argument (or, more exactly, on a series of arguments) from introspection. As an argument based on an introspective analysis of experience, it has the great virtue that anyone with normal intellectual powers can perform the introspective exercise and confirm the results for himself or herself. According to the Buddha's teaching, a careful introspective analysis reveals items belonging to the following – and only the following – categories, named *skandhas* in Sanskrit (Pāli: *khanda*), meaning 'bundle' or 'heap':

1. A physical body (Sanskrit and Pāli: *rūpa*).
2. Feeling (Sanskrit and Pāli: *vedanā*) (the hedonic tone of experience: pleasurable, painful, or neutral).
3. Interpretive perception (Pāli *saññā*, Sanskrit *saṃjñā*) (the mental processing of whatever is given within conscious awareness).
4. Mental formations/dispositions/tendencies (Pāli *saṅkhāra*, Sanskrit *saṃskāra*). This covers several processes – all thought to be carriers of *karma* – formative of character and having an influence on actions.
5. Consciousness (Pāli *viññāṇa*, Sanskrit *vijñāna*). This also carries *karma*. There are three modes of consciousness:
   - Pure awareness (abstract mental activity);
   - Mental activity with content (thought about physical or mental objects);
   - The mental functions of processing sense-data, judging, remembering and generally reasoning. (Adapted from Harrison (2019: 110))

This analysis of human persons in terms of the five *skandhas* has been at the core of Buddhist philosophy since its origins in the Buddha's teaching. The *skandhas* are listed in many early Buddhist texts, for example, the *Mahāsatipaṭṭhāna Sutta* (Walshe 1995: 342). See also the *Khandhasaṃyutta Sutta* 72, where the *skandhas* are more fully explained (Bodhi 2000: 914–18).

2.11 The Exhaustiveness Claim

Buddhist teachers invited would-be-disciples to try the introspective experiment for themselves. Students of Buddhism were challenged to find anything within their self-awareness that could not be classified as one of the five *skandhas*. The challenge is as difficult for people today as it must have been to contemporaries of the Buddha, for introspection does not reveal anything that cannot be classified as an example of one of the five *skandhas*. The *skandhas*, in other words, exhaust the possibilities. Mark Siderits has aptly labelled this the 'exhaustiveness claim' (Siderits 2007: 48–50).

A possible response to the exhaustiveness claim would be to say that, whatever the self is, it cannot be categorized as one of the *skandhas*. The self must not, therefore, be an object of possible human awareness. A Buddhist reply would be to point out that to posit a self that we cannot be aware of has no power at all to explain our experience.

Another possible response to the exhaustiveness claim would be to say that the self must be one of the five *skandhas*. As we see in the following section, this view is also problematic.

2.12 The Argument from Impermanence

Having established to his satisfaction that the list of five *skandhas* is exhaustive (because nothing else reveals itself to introspection), the Buddha went through the list asking if the phenomena within each category were permanent or impermanent. The answer for each one is the same: It is impermanent. If none of the *skandhas* are permanent, it follows that none of them can constitute a permanent, unchanging self. We would therefore say with respect to none of them 'this am I, this is my self' (Edelglass & Garfield 2009: 269). Once all five *skandhas* have been disqualified from constituting the self because of their impermanence, the argument from introspection that establishes the exhaustiveness claim is used to demonstrate that there is nothing else that the self could be. The conclusion of these arguments is that there is no self to be found.

This was not the end of the matter, however, for the Buddhist view faces a further objection. Some critics argued that, even if the exhaustiveness claim were correct, the five *skandhas* together might constitute a self. The Buddhist's reply took the form of an argument that a collection of impermanent things cannot come together to make something permanent and unchanging. They agreed, of course, that the *skandhas* do combine, thereby giving rise to the experience we all have of being persons with some measure of continuity through time. After all, the theory was proposed to explain our experience of personhood. The distinctive claim of early Buddhism was that whatever a human person is can be no more than the *skandhas* contribute. A human being just is a collection of parts – *skandhas* – arranged in a certain way.

2.13 No-Self

The conclusion that we do not have a permanent, unchanging, self is the core of the famous Buddhist theory of no-self (*anātman* in Sanskrit, *anattā* in Pāli). Notice that the Buddha is denying the existence of something very specific.

Namely, the permanent, unchanging *ātman* of the Brahmanical tradition. His theory is, therefore, not necessarily inconsistent with other views about what a human person might be. While the Buddha and his immediate followers seem to have been more concerned to demonstrate that the Brahmanical view of the self was false because unsupported, later philosophers in the Buddhist tradition sought to articulate an account of human persons that was consistent with the theory of no-self. Key to this account was the theory of conditioned co-arising.

2.14 Conditioned Co-Arising

As was explained in Section 2.12, early Buddhists argued that a collection of impermanent things cannot together constitute a permanent, unchanging whole. While this argument was originally deployed to refute a rival view about human persons, it soon began to be applied more widely to all entities. In Section 2.9, we saw that experience and reflection, on the Buddhist view, both tell us that nothing whatsoever exists permanently and unchangingly. They held that if something permanent and unchanging were to exist, it could neither have come into existence (for it must always have existed) nor go out of existence (because it cannot change). A core Buddhist conviction is that nothing exists in this way for everything is subject to change. This set of ideas has profound and far-reaching metaphysical implications, and the history of Buddhist philosophy is the story of the gradual working out of these.

The early Buddhists connected the idea of impermanence with the further idea of a lack of ontological independence. As we have seen, permanent, unchanging entities simply cannot be caused to exist because they always exist. The condition of such hypothetical entities is described as 'ontologically independent' because their existence would be independent of all external causes. A philosophical commitment agreed on by virtually all Buddhists is that nothing whatsoever possesses ontological independence. This denial that anything possesses ontological independence is also taken to apply to gods, and this constitutes one of the major disagreements between Buddhism and traditional Christianity (although McNabb and Baldwin (2022) argue that there is really no conflict here because classical theists do not hold God to be an entity, so such theists could agree with the Buddhist claim that all entities lack ontological independence).

Commitment to the experientially based idea that all entities are impermanent and lack ontological independence led early Buddhist philosophers to develop a metaphysical perspective according to which everything that comes to be is conditioned by what came before. In modern parlance, we would say that everything that comes to be exists contingently, and we would mean by this that if relevant conditions had been different the entity might not have come into being at all. The early Buddhists claimed that all phenomena arise interdependently. The Sanskrit term for the Buddhist theory is *pratītya samutpāda* (*paticca-samuppāda*, in Pāli). This term is often translated into English as conditioned co-arising. As we have seen, entities that are subject to conditioned co-arising lack ontological independence. The key point being asserted is that because all things arise in dependence on conditions outside themselves, nothing at all has ontological independence. We return to this key idea in Chapter 3.

2.15 Cessation

The theory of conditioned co-arising clarifies exactly what Buddhism denied about the existence of selves and other entities. In the light of this, we can return to the concept of *nirvāṇa*. As explained Section in 2.7, this Sanskrit term, which literally means 'extinction', refers to final release from *saṃsāra*. Buddhists deny that final *nirvāṇa* amounts to the annihilation of the self, so the English translation that best describes the Buddhist idea is 'cessation' rather than 'extinction'.

What happens when cessation occurs at the death of an awakened one? The following passage provides a convenient summary of the early Buddhist view. It is framed by the two opposite views rejected by early Buddhism: the view that the self continues to exist after the death of the material body and the view that the self is annihilated when the body dies.

> He, however, who abandons this knowledge of the truth and believes in a living entity must assume either that this living entity will perish or that it will not perish. If he assume that it will not perish, he falls into the heresy of the persistence of existences; or if he assume that it will perish, he falls into that of the annihilation of existences. And why do I say so? Because, just as sour cream has milk as its antecedent, so nothing here exists but what has its own antecedents. To say, 'The living entity persists', is to fall short of the truth; to say, 'It is annihilated', is to outrun the truth. (Radhakrishnan & Moore 1989: 285)

The most straightforward way to interpret this passage is as an attempt to divert discussion away from the traditional question of whether there is a self that survives the death of the body or not. The first sentence says that one who already believes in the existence of a self will have to hold one of two things: either that the self will perish when the body dies or that it will not. These claims are mutually exclusive (only one can be true) and exhaustive (there are no other options). The second sentence of the passage explains the consequences of each choice, although it does not provide arguments as these are well-rehearsed elsewhere. This statement and the one in the final sentence are useful because they give a clear account of the two views the Buddha rejected. His own teaching on human persons does not assume that the self is a living entity that could either persist or perish. The most significant sentence in the passage for understanding the early Buddhist view is this one: 'Because, just as sour cream has milk as its antecedent, so nothing here exists but what has its own antecedents.'

Suppose that you have a pot of sour cream in your refrigerator. You could ask yourself if it will continue to exist or perish, or you could consider how it came to be at all. The answer to the second question is that it had milk as its antecedent. In other words, had there been no milk, there would have been no sour cream. An obvious condition for the existence of sour cream is milk. The Buddha suggests that instead of asking whether the self persists or perishes when the body dies, we consider the antecedents of what we call the self. If we come to understand the conditions that give rise to our experience of persistence through time, we can then imagine those conditions having been absent, in which case the experience of the self would not have arisen. The Buddha taught that, ultimately, this understanding, when combined with meditation and practice of the ethical elements of the eightfold path, will allow us to prevent further arising. This is what early Buddhists regarded as cessation, *nirvāṇa*.

3 Being and Emptiness

Having introduced the core Buddhist ideas of impermanence (*anitya / anicca*), suffering (*duḥkha / dukkha*), no-self (*anātman / anattā*), conditioned co-arising (*pratītya samutpāda / paticca-samuppāda*), and cessation (*nirvāṇa / nibbāna*), we are now positioned to understand the key philosophical differences that developed between Brahmanical and Buddhist schools (as well as between different brands of Buddhist philosophy). Arguments concerning being and emptiness are the focus of this chapter. The arguments to be considered all concern the concept *svabhāva* (*sabhāva* in Pāli), about which there is no consensus on how to translate into English most appropriately. Some of the options are 'own-being', 'independent existence', 'intrinsic nature', and 'essence'. For reasons to be explained in Section 3.3, my preference is to translate *svabhāva* as 'own-being'. Whichever translation is used, the arguments which developed in clusters around the concept of *svabhāva* in India, and around closely related issues in China, provide a window onto the key concerns shaping major Indian and Chinese traditions of religious philosophy during the first millennium of the Common Era. As was suggested earlier (Section 1.3), these shared concerns allow us to regard the Asian traditions considered in this Element as involved in a common philosophical project.

The issues can be approached by first focusing on two dichotomies which seem naturally to present themselves when people think about existence. While most, and possibly all, entities within our experience exist contingently (in the sense that they might not have existed and may cease to exist), most of us can at least understand what it would be like for something to exist necessarily. Entities that exist contingently are not the cause of their own existence, they are ontologically dependent (that is, dependent for their being) on something extrinsic to themselves. An entity that exists necessarily is ontologically independent, in the sense that its being is not dependent on anything extrinsic to itself. The distinction between ontologically dependent contingent existence and ontologically independent necessary existence forms our first dichotomy. The second dichotomy is between permanence and impermanence. The two dichotomies are closely related because the second is implied by the first, for non-permanence is included in the concept of contingent existence and permanence is included in the concept of necessary existence.

There is a vast literature on contingency and necessity within Western philosophy, as these have been key concepts within metaphysics since the mediaeval period (see Hale (2013) and Leftow (2022) for examples of recent work on this topic). It is often overlooked, however, that the contrast between contingency and necessity, regarded as two modes of existence, frames many of the metaphysical systems of the ancient world. It is no less central to early and mediaeval Jewish, Christian, and Muslim philosophies (consider, for instance, the works of Anselm of Canterbury, Thomas Aquinas, Moses Maimonides, and Ibn Sina) than it is to Asian religious philosophy – but this is a story that will not be told here. The ubiquity of the dichotomies between, on the one hand, ontologically independent necessary existence and ontologically dependent contingent existence and, on the other hand, permanence and impermanence can thus provide a conceptual bridge between otherwise very different metaphysical systems. This Element uses this bridge to show how Indian and Chinese philosophy meet each other with shared concerns.

In both India and China, reflection on the package of ideas connected to the two dichotomies introduced above led to the conclusion that anything possessing ontologically independent necessary existence and, therefore, permanence must lack parts. The argument was that having parts would imply that the existence of the entity was dependent on the existence of its individual parts, so composite entities could not be regarded as ontologically independent. As will be explained in Section 3.9, this line of reflection supported monist views about the ontological foundation of reality (that is, views holding that, at the most fundamental level, reality is one thing lacking real differentiation). Monist views are found in the works of a wide variety of thinkers across the world (Ivanhoe et al. 2018), and such views are especially associated with Advaita Vedānta Hinduism (Frazier 2022), Yogācāra Buddhism (Siderits 2007: Chapter 7), and Lu-Wang neo-Confucianism (Ivanhoe 2009). In all these philosophical traditions, to lack parts meant not only that an entity was materially non-composite but also that it was temporally non-composite. That which is ontologically independent and permanent was regarded as a non-spatial and non-temporal whole.

Monism about the ontological foundation of reality was not, however, the only position to emerge from reflection on modes of existence. A rival view held that reality had no ontological foundation, for insofar as anything existed at all its existence could only be contingent and non-permanent (see Section 2.14). This led to the claim that came to characterize Mahāyāna Buddhism, that all beings, or all phenomena, are empty (see Section 3.4).

3.1 Outline

After providing some essential information on the textual sources for the philosophies to be covered, this chapter introduces the great Buddhist philosopher and saint Nāgārjuna (c. 150–c. 250 CE). Just as the Buddha had changed the framework in which many people thought about the self and the cycle of rebirth (see Section 2.6), Nāgārjuna developed a radically new framework for thinking about being and non-being that had profound spiritual implications (see Westerhoff (2009) for an accessible introduction). Nāgārjuna's framework was widely adopted, and it was later adapted by different branches of Mahāyāna Buddhism in Tibet, China, Korea, and Japan. After explaining the early Mahāyāna perspective, the chapter brings it into conversation with the contrasting perspective of the Hindu philosopher Śaṅkara (c. 650–c. 800 CE),[7] who developed a form of monism that was indebted to Buddhist thought (King 1997). The topic of monism provides an entry point to ideas that became prominent in China, these are introduced in Section 3.8 in preparation for Chapter 4, which focuses on Chinese philosophers and classical Chinese religious-philosophical texts.

3.2 Texts

Like all pre-modern works, the texts discussed in this chapter benefit from being read with a modern commentary. It is not always easy for a modern reader, without appropriate training, to distinguish between when an author is stating an

[7] Śaṅkara is a transliteration of the Sanskrit शङ्कर, an alternative transliteration is Śaṃkara.

opponent's position to later refute it or when an author is explaining their own view. The practice of seamlessly weaving incompatible philosophical positions into a dense set of sūtras was a heuristic device to aid memorization; a modern reader, however, can easily come away from such texts with the impression that the author is guilty of blatant self-contradiction. Learning to read ancient texts carefully is a vital step in coming to understand Asian philosophical traditions. In addition to their internal complexity, further difficulties are caused by lack of secure information about the context and date of the composition of key texts, whose authorship is often also uncertain.

The most important collection of Mahāyāna Buddhist sūtras is *The Perfection of Wisdom Sūtras* (*Prajñāpāramitā*). These sūtras were compiled over many centuries from the turn of the Common Era and the earliest show us the new wave of philosophical creativity within Buddhist thought that was key to the emergence of Mahāyāna Buddhism in its various forms. *The Heart of Wisdom Sūtra* (*Prajñāpāramitāhṛdaya Sūtra*) (see Section 3.7) is the most well known of *The Perfection of Wisdom Sūtras*, as it contains the quintessential expression of Mahāyāna teaching on emptiness and form (see Pine (2005) for an English translation). Buddhist tradition holds this text to have originated in India; however, a growing number of scholars hold that its origins are in China. In addition to lack of agreement about the origin of *The Heart of Wisdom Sūtra*, and despite its importance, there is also a lack of consensus on its date of composition.

The Flower Ornament Sūtra (*Avataṃsaka Sūtra*) is another important text for Chinese Buddhism. Many different Chinese translations of this Sanskrit text are still in circulation today (see Cleary (1993) for an accessible English translation). It is one of the most influential Buddhist texts in East Asia and is the foundational scripture of an influential form of Chinese Buddhism known as Hua Yan (華嚴). See Liu (2006) for an excellent introduction to the main schools of Chinese Buddhist philosophy.

In *The Fundamental Wisdom of the Middle Way* (*Mūlamadhyamakakārikā*), Nāgārjuna sets out the early Mahāyāna teaching on emptiness and form and articulates his stance on the emptiness of emptiness. See Garfield (1995) for a translation and commentary. Key ideas from Nāgārjuna's text are discussed in Sections 3.6 and 3.7.

The Ornament of the Middle Way (*Madhyamakālaṃkāra*) is an important text within Tibetan Buddhism that probably originated in the eighth century CE. It is thought to have been originally composed in Sanskrit by Śāntarakṣita in the first wave of the transmission of Buddhism into Tibet. It now exists only in Tibetan. See Blumenthal (2004) for a translation and discussion.

Śaṅkara's most famous work is a commentary on the *Brahma Sūtra* (which is sometimes known as the *Vedānta Sūtra*). See *Brahma Sūtra Bhāṣya of*

Shankaracharya, translated by S. Gambhirananda (1965).[8] See Mayeda (1992) for an accessible translation of Śaṅkara's key teachings with a modern commentary.

3.3 *Svabhāva*

The debate about being and emptiness within Indian philosophy concerned how to understand the nature of ourselves and our reality. This was by no means an abstract philosophical debate, for it was framed by the overriding spiritual concern to deal with the suffering caused by rebirth by breaking its deadly cycle. As was explained in Section 3.1, *svabhāva* was the most important concept used to articulate the core issues at stake in this debate. The lexical root of this Sanskrit term is *bhāva*, which means 'being', and its prefix *sva* means 'self'. A literal translation of *svabhāva* would, then, be 'self-being'. This literal translation does not, however, reveal the full complexity of the concept.

The first step to understanding the deeper meaning of *svabhāva* is to consider its opposite, *parabhāva*, which literally translates as 'other-being'. An entity whose mode of existence can be characterized as *parabhāva*, other-being, depends on another for its coming into being and for its remaining in being, such an entity is ontologically dependent. In contrast to this, an entity whose mode of existence can be characterized as *svabhāva*, self-being, does not depend on another for its coming into being or for its remaining in being, such an entity is ontologically independent. The core distinction between these two modes of being, then, is that one mode – *svabhāva* – is characterized by ontological independence, whereas the other mode – *parabhāva* – is characterized by ontological dependence. This is a crucial distinction to keep in mind when interpreting Indian philosophical texts, especially those from Buddhist and Advaita Vedānta traditions.

No convenient English term adequately expresses the full range of meanings carried by the Sanskrit *svabhāva*. This is largely because, as Jay Garfield notes, none of the most obvious potential translations – such as, nature, substance, or essence – come with a contrasting term that captures what is most important: namely, that any entity possessing *svabhāva* is independent of anything external to itself for its existence and its nature (Garfield 2015: 61). Because of this problem, most commentators either leave *svabhāva* untranslated or employ one of the hybrid terms that have been specially coined to express its meaning in English: 'own-being', 'own-nature', 'self-being', and 'self-nature'. Of these four, the first – 'own-being' – is the least problematic. 'Own-nature' risks importing views about what it is to have a nature, 'self-being' does the same

[8] https://archive.org/details/brahma-sutra-bhasya-of-sankaracharya-swami-gambhirananda.

with respect to 'self', and 'self-nature' carries the risks attendant on both its terms. 'Own-being' comes closest to capturing the key idea that an entity characterizable as *svabhāva* is ontologically independent, being the source (and sustainer) of its own being. Noting that the key idea that if any being were to be accurately characterized as *svabhāva*, that being would be ontologically independent is included in none of the possible English translations, this Element will translate *svabhāva* as 'own-being' in those cases when the word is not left untranslated.

Garfield prefers to translate *svabhāva* with the compound term 'intrinsic nature' because, by doing so, we can at least contrast 'intrinsic' and 'extrinsic'. The difficulty with this choice, however, is that to ascribe the property of having an intrinsic nature to an entity does not by itself tell us anything about how that entity came to possess that intrinsic nature, nor does it tell us anything about how the entity maintains its intrinsic nature. In other words, the key idea of ontological independence is not (or, at least, not obviously) included in the concept of intrinsic nature. A further difficulty is caused by regarding *svabhāva* as if it were a single property, or even a cluster of properties. I suggest that rather than focus on properties, it is helpful to think about *svabhāva* and its contrasting term *parabhāva* as denoting two modes of existence. Properties, such as permanence, can then be understood as derivative on these modes of existence. Thus, an entity characterizable as *svabhāva* would possess the properties of ontological independence, necessary existence, and permanence, while an entity characterizable as *parabhāva* would possess the properties of ontological dependence, contingent existence, and impermanence. So, to say that an entity lacks *svabhāva*, own-being, means primarily that it does not enjoy a certain mode of existence, and secondarily that it lacks the properties of ontological independence, necessary existence, and permanence. While the strategy of focusing on modes of existence may not work well in all contexts where the terms *svabhāva* and *parabhāva* are used, it at least has the virtue of making the core philosophical issues that are at stake stand out more clearly.

We can now express the most important question by emphasizing modes of existence rather than properties: Does anything enjoy the *svabhāvic* mode of existence? In the following section, we look at some answers to this question proposed by Buddhist philosophers.

3.4 Buddhist Ontology

Despite their many other differences, virtually all Buddhist philosophers are united in the view that our experience does not bring us into contact with anything which enjoys ontological independence. Within the style of Buddhist philosophy that came to ascendency in India prior to the Common Era, namely, Abhidharma Buddhism, consensus developed that all the entities that we directly encounter within our everyday experience are composite macro-entities that can be conceptually analysed into very small component parts, named *dharmas*. These *dharmas* were thought to be outside the range of our possible experience. Macro-entities, such as persons, elephants, and houses, in this early Buddhist view, cannot be characterized as in possession of own-being. No composite entities can enjoy the *svabhāvic* mode of existence for one obvious reason: they depend, both for their coming into existence and for their continuing in existence, on their micro-constituent parts. Human persons, for instance, just like elephants, depend on both physical and mental parts (see Section 2.10), whereas houses depend on different types of material constituents organized in a certain configuration to form rooms, doors, and windows. It is notable that this early Buddhist position could be consistently held alongside the view that the micro-constituents (the *dharmas*) could enjoy the *svabhāvic* mode of existence. Indeed, important strands of early Buddhist thought seem to have accepted that the micro-entities that formed the ultimate constituents of the things we experience at the macro-level were permanent and indestructible.[9] In conversation with the Brahmanical philosophical traditions, however, the view gradually disappeared that *dharmas* could be correctly characterized as existing in the *svabhāvic* mode. While they did not deny the conceptual coherence of the *svabhāvic* mode of existence, Buddhists (unlike others among their Indian contemporaries) came to hold that nothing at all existed in this way.

As we have seen, the Buddhist position gradually settled into the view that the coming into being of anything is the result of a complex network of causal conditions (Section 2.14). Beings arise as a result of background conditions, and they cease to be when their sustaining conditions change in a relevant way. This teaching is sometimes misinterpreted as the claim that nothing really exists and that our experience comprehensively misleads us into believing that people, water, trees, and so on, are real. Such ontological nihilism, as it has been called, is not found in the early Buddhist material. Early Buddhists did not deny the existence of the entities we take ourselves to experience. Their claims, rather, concerned how the entities we experience come to be and what explains their cessation. Their conclusion was that the existence of entities is dependent on factors extrinsic to themselves. In other words, all entities can be characterized as existing in the *parabhāvic* mode; they possess the properties of impermanence and ontological dependence.

[9] Similar ideas can be found in pre-Socratic Greek philosophy. Consider, for instance, Democritus' idea of the atom.

During the first few centuries of the Common Era, the early Buddhist view was radicalized by philosophers under the influence of Nāgārjuna known as Mādhyamikas (who were so called because they worked in the Madhyamaka tradition). Building on the teaching of the *Heart of Wisdom Sūtra*, Mādhyamikas came to deny not only that anything enjoyed the *svabhāvic* mode of existence but also that anything enjoyed the *parabhāvic* mode of existence. According to this way of thinking, there simply are no *svabhāvic* or *parabhāvic* entities. In fact, these two concepts seem to have been reinterpreted by bringing them into relation to the two opposite views about the self that were denied by earlier Buddhists, namely, either that the self will perish when the body dies or that it will not (see Section 2.15). Mādhyamikas proposed a middle way between the two opposite and 'extreme' views, thus claiming to bring Buddhist teaching more into line with the Buddha's original intention. The Mādhyamikas, then, popularized the view that all phenomeona lack *bhava* – being. This claim covered both *svabhāva* and *parabhāva*. The denial of the latter sharply distinguishes this position from the one advocated by earlier schools of Buddhism, and it provided the Mādhyamikas grounds for the claim that they were returning to the Buddha's original teaching rather than propounding a new philosophy.

Nonetheless, the Mādhyamikas' claim that they were merely restating the Buddha's original teaching was rather disingenuous, for the radical consequence of their handling of the notions of *svabhāva* and *parabhāva* was the view that no entities ever arose or ceased. According to this Madhyamaka interpretation of the Buddha's teaching, there are no entities. This explains why philosophers who adopt this perspective prefer to refer to phenomena rather than entities. The term 'phenomena' can be used to describe anything within human experience without thereby committing its user to the claim that there is an entity that could be characterized as either *svabhāvic* or *parabhāvic* (as these were taken to be mutually exclusive and exhaustive modes of existence, any entity that was found to exist would have to be enjoying one or the other of these modes of existence).

Nāgārjuna is the most well-known and influential early exponent of the Madhyamaka perspective. He changed the parameters of the debate about being and non-being by giving a central place to the concept of emptiness (*śūnyatā*) (Burton 2014). From this point on, the Mādhyamikas' thinking about being and becoming, arising and ceasing was framed by their understanding of *śūnyatā*. Later we examine a Hindu expression of the opposite view, one that reached maturity in the work of the Advaitin philosopher Śaṅkara, with his conception of *nirguṇa Brahman* (qualityless Brahman), which is indebted to earlier Buddhist reflections on emptiness (King 1997). Before doing so, we take a closer look at Nāgārjuna's understanding of what it means for all phenomena to be *svabhāva-śūnya* (empty of own-being).

3.5 *Svabhāva-Śūnya*

As was explained in Section 3.4, the Mādhyamikas hold that neither macroscopic nor microscopic entities enjoy the *svabhāvic* mode of existence. Nāgārjuna's insight was that all phenomena, not just the macroscopic phenomena that are large enough for us to experience, are interdependently arisen and hence not *svabhāvic*. According to Nāgārjuna, all phenomena are empty (*śūnya*) of own-being (*svabhāva*). Notice that, unlike earlier Buddhists, Nāgārjuna does not claim that non-*svabhāvic* beings are *parabhāvic*. His view is that phenomena are neither *svabhāvic* nor *parabhāvic* because *bhava* (being) is a concept without instantiation. This is Nāgārjuna's well-known theory of emptiness (*śūnyatā*). Chapter 24, verse 19 of his *Fundamental Verses on the Middle Way* reads:

> There does not exist anything
> That is not dependently arisen.
> Therefore there does not exist anything
> That is not empty. (Garfield 2015: 64)

Nāgārjuna's theory is sometimes characterized as a form of ontological nihilism, understood as the sweeping view that nothing at all exists. Ascribing such a view to Nāgārjuna is not, however, supported by textual evidence and is inconsistent with Nāgārjuna's overall position (Garfield 2014). To understand Nāgārjuna's position properly, it needs to be carefully distinguished from the claim that nothing exists. No Buddhist philosophers have ever supported the claim that nothing exists! Rather, Buddhist philosophies are all concerned to offer an analysis of existents (or phenomena) as dependently arisen. Nāgārjuna is no exception to this. To understand him (or any other Buddhist philosopher), it is helpful to start by asking what is being identified as the object of negation. In Nāgārjuna's case, the object of negation is not existence but *svabhāvic* existence. In other words, he is denying that any entity exists *svabhāvically* and, thereby, claiming that nothing possesses the properties of permanence and ontological independence.

Nāgārjuna's theory of emptiness is also prone to misinterpretation by commentators who bring to the discussion the assumption that *svabhāva* means intrinsic nature (Garfield 2015: 65). If *svabhāva* could be adequately translated as intrinsic nature, then *svabhāva-śūnya* could be rendered as 'empty of intrinsic nature'. This interpretation, however, would lose sight of the vital contrast between whether what causes something to be and sustains that thing in being is extrinsic or intrinsic to that thing or not. One problem is that none of the standard understandings of intrinsic nature available within Western philosophy are tethered to a view about the original or sustaining cause of the being that is said to possesses intrinsic nature. Consequently, from a Western philosophical perspective, to deny that an entity has an intrinsic nature is not equivalent to denying that it is the cause of its own being.

The key point denied by early Buddhist philosophers was that *any* entity is ontologically independent of factors extrinsic to itself. Because of this, within Buddhist thought, lack of an intrinsic nature is more accurately regarded as resulting from ontological dependence rather than being a primary fact to be understood in isolation from the more fundamental issue. Interestingly, as we have seen, early Buddhists standardly accepted that ontological independence – the *svabhāvic* mode of existence – was metaphysically and conceptually possible; they simply denied on both empirical and analytical grounds that any entity was in this condition.

Prior to Nāgārjuna, the dominant view within Buddhist philosophy was that all entities arise in dependence on others. After Nāgārjuna, the language typically used by Indian, and later by Chinese and Tibetan, Buddhist philosophers began to shift away from talk about beings or entities and causal dependency towards discourse focused on phenomena arising and the conditions of that arising. To put the matter bluntly, according to this view, beings are neither originated dependently nor independently – for there are no beings, as such, only phenomena.

The obvious philosophical differences between the teachings of the Buddha and his early followers and those of Nāgārjuna and his followers reveal an interesting feature that seems to be built into the core of Buddhist thought. Buddhism's basic teachings, especially that of conditioned co-arising (Section 2.14), skilful means (Section 3.7), and the theory of two truths (Section 3.7), encourage doctrinal innovation and the continual adaptation of the teaching to new environments. In effect, Buddhism has no final teaching, and this has allowed for its philosophical fecundity and its ability to take root and transform itself in the context of cultures very different from that of its original Indian home. Early Buddhism's transition into its various Mahāyāna forms witnesses to this extraordinary versatility. *Mahā* means 'great' and *yana* means 'means to' (in the sense of 'vehicle'), Mahāyāna, then, can be translated as the 'Great Means to Liberation' – and it is a means that is continuously expanding to meet new contexts.

3.6 Non-Duality

The Mādhyamikas' claim that there are no beings but only phenomena, although it was derived from early Buddhist teaching, marked a significant departure from all previous Buddhist philosophy (see Section 3.5). As we will see later, it also provided a starting point for the development of other significant Mahāyāna traditions of the philosophical interpretation of Buddhism (one of which being the Yogācāra, or Cittamātra – Mind Only – school; see Section 3.9).

The immediate and obvious consequence of Nāgārjuna's view was, however, the insertion of a theory of non-duality into Buddhism. The claim that there are no beings, or entities, only phenomena, was ontologically levelling. Everything that falls within the range of our possible or actual experience, according to this theory, is an arisen phenomenon. Nothing is more real than anything else. This raises the question of what differentiates an awakened one's experiences from those of ordinary un-awakened persons. Nāgārjuna's most radical claim was that 'There is not the slightest difference between cyclic existence and nirvāṇa. There is not the slightest difference between nirvāṇa and cyclic existence' (Garfield 1995: 75). An awakened one, therefore, experiences the same world as everyone else. Those who are awakened do not somehow escape to a realm where beings enjoy existence in the *svabhāvic* mode.

Realizing the truth of Buddhism, according to Nāgārjuna, involves, first, understanding that all beings are empty (*śūnya*) of own-being (*svabhāva*) and, second, understanding, what he called, the emptiness of emptiness (*śūnyatā-śūnya*). It is Nāgārjuna's commitment to the emptiness of emptiness that makes twentieth-century interpretations of him as an ontological nihilist untenable. His claim that emptiness is empty can be interpreted as the claim that emptiness makes no difference to the phenomenology of experience; likewise, his claim that there is no distinction between *saṃsāra* and *nirvāṇa* is not a denial that either *saṃsāra* or *nirvāṇa* can be experienced. Nāgārjuna's philosophy is profoundly positive, which belies the common assumption that Buddhism is a pessimistic philosophy whose core teaching concerns the inevitability of suffering. In his own day, Nāgārjuna's account of *svabhāva-śūnya* in terms of the emptiness of emptiness provided a fresh perspective on the Buddha's message that the solution to the problem of human suffering had been found.

3.7 The Emptiness of Emptiness

Nāgārjuna's conception of the emptiness of emptiness (*śūnyatā-śūnya*) was framed within Buddhism's teaching about 'two truths', which was originally used to reconcile what appeared to be inconsistencies between some of the statements attributed to the Buddha. In some of the Buddha's discourses, for example, there are references to selves, even though the Buddha taught that there are none such. The Buddha was evidently skilful at adapting the presentation of his teaching to his audience by saying different things to different people depending on their individual needs and level of understanding. Buddhists have a technical term to describe this pedagogical practice: *upāya*, or skilful means. The idea of 'two truths' was also used to deal with the fact that slightly varying accounts of the Buddha's teaching were passed down through different oral traditions. Considering that the Buddha had a teaching career spanning forty-five years, during which he taught many groups and individuals in a wide variety of places, slight discrepancies in the oral traditions are unsurprising. Given the Buddha's practice of adapting his teaching to his audience combined with the variety of environments in which he taught, it was impossible for later Buddhists to make all the Buddha's utterances consistent. The effort to systematize the Buddha's teaching eventually led to the claim that there are two types of truth.

Conventional truth is thought to be what people generally agree to be true about the everyday world. The Sanskrit term for conventional truth is *saṃvṛti-satya*. *Satya* means 'truth' and *saṃvṛti* qualifies what kind of truth is at issue. *Saṃvṛti* is a significant choice of word with which to characterize this type of truth, for, in addition to its primary meaning of conventional truth or truth by agreement, it has a secondary meaning. Surprisingly, the secondary meaning is suggestive of something hidden. Conventional truth, then, is a type of truth that conceals rather than reveals. What it conceals is ultimate truth, known in Sanskrit as *paramārtha-satya*, which is truth that tells us how things really are.

The distinction between two types of truth can be applied to many facets of the Buddha's teaching. It can be used, for example, to interpret the Buddha's different statements about selves along the following lines: When the Buddha's teaching includes talk of selves who have moral responsibility, what he says is held to be true at the conventional level. When the Buddha explains that really there are neither selves nor moral responsibility, what he says is held to be true at the ultimate level. The distinction between two types of truth allowed the Buddha's followers to reconcile these two sets of claims.

Different views arose within Buddhism about how the two types of truth are related (Zhao 2022: 189–91). The dominant view prior to Nāgārjuna was that conventional truths could be reduced to ultimate ones through philosophical analysis, and the entities to which conventional truths appeared to refer could likewise be eliminated from a correct ontology (Thakchöe 2007). This reflected a straightforward distinction between the way things appear to be conventionally and the ultimate truth about the way they are. Sometimes this distinction was understood as the claim that reality can be conceptualized by means of two different perspectives, one ultimate and one conventional. From the conventional perspective, a human person, for example, *appears* to grow from a child to an adult then to age and die, but from an ultimate perspective there is no human person only the five *skandhas*.

Nāgārjuna revolutionized the way the relation between the two types of truth was understood when he rejected the previously dominant view, claiming instead that there was no substantial distinction between them. This claim resulted in dramatic changes to the way other core doctrines of Buddhism were interpreted and presented (Garfield 2015). Nāgārjuna's bold claim that 'the boundary of *nirvāṇa* is also the boundary of *saṃsāra*, there is not even a subtle difference between them' (*The Fundamental Wisdom of the Middle Way*, chapter 25, stanzas 19–20, in King (1999: 124)), which amounted to a vision of reality as a unified whole (see Section 3.6), was a consequence of his recasting of the teaching on two truths. Nāgārjuna favoured neither reduction nor elimination of *saṃsāra* (the phenomenal world) to *nirvāṇa* holding that both strategies were neither analytically possible nor desirable. Ontological non-duality (see Section 3.6) thus maps onto Nāgārjuna's commitment to the view that the so-called two truths are ultimately one and the same.

Prior to the rise of Nāgārjuna's Madhyamaka philosophical perspective, Buddhist teaching and meditative practices served to foster discrimination between the appearance of our everyday world that was captured in statements of conventional truth and the ultimate reality expressed in ultimate truth. As we have seen, it was precisely this distinction that was dissolved by Nāgārjuna (and others in the Madhyamaka tradition) when they denied that the world as it appears to us is reductively analysable to a more ultimate level. After Nāgārjuna, philosophers could still engage in analysis provided they recognized that analysis does not entail reduction or elimination because there is no privileged level of fundamental ultimate reality to which truths about the conventional world could be reduced. This is the doctrine of the emptiness of emptiness, the quintessential expression of which is found in *The Heart of Wisdom Sūtra* (Pine 2005), which is the first text of (arguably) Chinese origin to be discussed in this Element. Here is the key stanza:

> Form is empty.
> Emptiness is form.
> Form is not other than emptiness.
> Emptiness is not other than form. (Garfield 2015: 63)

In this passage, 'form' stands for phenomena, the stuff that populates the conventional everyday world of our experience. It is this that the first line tells us is empty of *svabhāva*. Phenomena do not arise independently. The second line is a statement against the view that our analysis of phenomena reveals an ultimate reality 'emptiness' underlying them. Emptiness is not a separate ontological substratum; rather, it is nothing other than the phenomena that arise and cease within our experience. Reading lines 1 and 3, and 2 and 4, together makes these points even more clearly:

Form is empty.
Form is not other than emptiness.
Emptiness is form.
Emptiness is not other than form.

Lines 1 and 3 teach that phenomena are empty, for analysis reveals that there is no more to them than emptiness. Correspondingly, lines 2 and 4 stress that emptiness just is phenomenal appearance and there is nothing more to it than that. As Jay Garfield sums up the view: 'To be a conventional phenomenon is to be empty; to be empty is to be merely conventionally real. The ultimate reality of things (their emptiness) and the fact that they are merely conventionally real are the same thing' (Garfield 2015: 63). The distinctions between conventional and ultimate reality and conventional and ultimate truth have been transcended by rejection of the presupposition that was widely held by philosophers prior to Nāgārjuna that ultimate reality was, by definition, reality that possesses *svabhāva*. Nāgārjuna's great intellectual innovation lay in his conviction that nothing enjoys the *svabhāvic* mode of existence at either the conventional or the ultimate level. It was this conviction that led him to reject the previously taken for granted distinction between two types of truth, the conventional and the ultimate, in favour of a non-dualist view which took all reality to be on the same level. While we can still understand reality from a conventional or from an ultimate perspective, the emptiness of emptiness teaching is that these two perspectives are really one.

It is difficult to overestimate how influential Nāgārjuna's teaching, as it is transmitted through the lines quoted above from *The Heart of Wisdom Sūtra*, has been on South and East Asian religion and philosophy.[10] To give just one example, Chinese Chan Buddhism, which is the predecessor of Zen Buddhism (Cleary 1998), developed through an extrapolation on the perspective on emptiness found in this sūtra.

[10] Given the uncertainties about the origin and dating of *The Heart of Wisdom Sūtra*, which were noted in Section 3.2, combined with uncertainties about Nāgārjuna's biography, it is impossible to say with certainty which came first. While the original composition of *The Heart of Wisdom Sūtra* may well predate Nāgārjuna, Buddhist tradition closely associates Nāgārjuna's teaching on the emptiness of emptiness with this sūtra.

3.8 Emptiness and Interpenetration

Other important Buddhist philosophical traditions built on the foundations laid by the Mādhyamikas, notably Yogācāra Buddhism (which was at a high point in the fourth century CE) and Hua Yan Buddhism (which emerged in the sixth century CE in China).

Yogācāra is alternatively known as *Cittamātra* (Mind Only), *Vijñaptimātra* (Consciousness Only), and *Vijñānavāda* (the Way of Consciousness). All these names well represent the focus of this strand of Buddhism on an analysis of consciousness. While there are two different streams within Yogācāra, one emphasizing the phenomenology of conscious experience and the other emphasizing consciousness as the unity underpinning the multiplicity of phenomena, Yogācāra as a whole can be interpreted as complementary to earlier Madhyamaka thought, for its analysis of subjectivity supplements the Mādhyamikas' analysis of phenomena.

One view of the relationship between the teachings of Yogācāra and Madhyamaka is that the former can be read as giving a correct account of conventional reality/truth which prepares the mind for the ultimate truth taught by the Mādhyamikas. This is the view that, through the influence of Śāntarakṣita, has been accepted in the Tibetan tradition since the ninth century CE. Here is the key passage:

> On the basis of Yogācāra,
> One should understand the absence of external objects.
> On the basis of our system [Madhyamaka],
> One should understand that there is also a complete absence of self.
> Whoever rides the chariot of these two systems.
> Guiding them with the reigns of logic,
> Will thereby attain the goal,
> The realization of the Mahāyāna itself.
>
> (*The Ornament of the Middle Way,* translation in Garfield (2015: 82))

Śāntarakṣita's explanation of the relation between the two strands of Mahāyāna philosophy is compelling. It not only gives an account of their compatibility but also serves as a corrective to an extension of the Yogācāra view that seemed to imply that Mind or Consciousness was the one ultimate reality. This extreme version of Yogācāra was incompatible with both the Madhyamaka teaching on the emptiness of emptiness and the Mādhyamaka's commitment to the view that there is no ultimate ontological ground to what we conventionally regard as real.

As we have seen, the main insight fuelling both Madhyamaka and Yogācāra is that emptiness is the consequence of the fact that phenomena are neither self-generating nor self-sustaining, but arise when conditions are right for their arising. A further philosophical development of this insight is found in *The Flower Ornament Sūtra*, the main sūtra of the Hua Yan tradition. In this sūtra, which many regard as the finest philosophical expression of Mahāyāna Buddhism, the interdependence of all phenomena was taken to imply that there are no discrete individuals and that everything is related to everything else. Hua Yan Buddhists concluded from this that all phenomena are constituted by relations and so they form a unity (on Hua Yan, see Liu (2006: Chapter 10)). As Garfield sums up this development: 'Emptiness here, just as in Indian Madhyamaka, is a lack of independent existence. But it is more than that. It is a lack of *difference* between entities' (Garfield 2015: 76). With the qualification that it is more accurate to refer to phenomena than entities, the point remains that for Hua Yan 'all is one' (Garfield 2015: 76).

3.9 All Is One

While all the major Buddhist schools of the Common Era consolidated their view that no phenomena enjoyed *svabhāvic* existence (see Section 3.3), the opposite view gradually gained ground among non-Buddhist philosophers in India through the influence of Śaṅkara's compelling presentation of the Hindu philosophy of Advaita Vedānta. Like Hua Yan Buddhism in China, Advaita Vedānta taught that a correct understanding of the nature of reality is monist. Section 1 concludes with a brief introduction to Śaṅkara's view before turning again to Chinese traditions in Section 4.

As is the case with many extremely well-known philosophers from the pre-modern Sanskrit intellectual world, despite his importance there is a great deal of uncertainty about the details of Śaṅkara's biography. Prior to modernity, biographical details were rarely recorded as the personal identity of authors was not thought to be of particular importance. All we can say is that Śaṅkara probably came from a South Indian Brahmanical family and probably lived sometime between 650 and 800 CE (see Suthren Hirst (2005) for an illuminating reconstruction of Śaṅkara's biography that relates it to the content and manner of his teaching). Śaṅkara is often credited with formulating a Hindu response to Buddhism and thereby beginning the period of Hindu resurgence that corresponded to the eclipse of Buddhism within India. While this may be exaggerated, Śaṅkara's philosophical system certainly merits careful attention for the way it engaged with the current intellectual issues of his day – especially those concerning the nature of being and becoming. Śaṅkara's response to Buddhism is also notable as an example of philosophical synthesis, for it was indebted to Buddhist reflections on *svabhāva* (King 1997).

As a philosopher in the ancient tradition of Vedānta, Śaṅkara's heritage was in the Vedas, the Upaniṣads (about which see Section 2.3), and in the later more devotional text, the *Bhagavad-gītā* (Prabhavananda & Isherwood 2002). In his elucidation of the Vedic tradition, Śaṅkara attempted to bring consistency into his interpretation of the ancient material by employing a version of the theory of two truths which, as we have seen, was widely used by Buddhist philosophers. In Śaṅkara's system, the distinction between two types of truth – the conventional and the ultimate – was mapped onto two types of reality. Conventional reality was taken to be the world of our everyday experience, while ultimate reality was regarded as that on which conventional reality depended. Those who, like Śaṅkara, took this distinction to concern ontology rather than perspective agreed that if anything were to exist non-conventionally, it would enjoy the *svabhāvic* mode of existence – being the source of its own being and nature, and existing outside the realm of change. The key difference between the Buddhist positions and Śaṅkara's lies in the latter's assessment that ultimate reality is not empty: the *svabhāvic* mode of existence is instantiated.

Śaṅkara's name for ultimate reality, the single ground of the universe, is *nirguṇa Brahman*. The term *nirguṇa*, however, signifies that this reality is without properties (*Brahma Sūtra Bhāṣya*, 3.2.18, Sankaracarya (1965)). In Śaṅkara's view, *svabhāva* is a term that in our conventional way of speaking tells us what *nirguṇa Brahman* is not. We cannot give any positive characterization of *nirguṇa Brahman*, which entails that it is not accessible to human reason. It should be noted that *nirguṇa Brahman* is not regarded by Śaṅkara as a personal God. To be personal would require that a God had at least some properties. Of course, Śaṅkara had to use some words to characterize *nirguṇa Brahman*, and the terms he used most frequently were 'being' and 'consciousness' (see *Brahma Sūtra Bhāṣya*, 3.2.21, for example). These terms provided the mind with objects for meditation but were not meant to be literal descriptions of the ultimately real.

The view that ultimate reality is without properties is difficult to sustain because it raises both philosophical and religious difficulties. Śaṅkara remained committed to it because of his conviction that if anything were to exist *svabhāvically*, it must be a unity, and unities, by definition, lack parts. As we saw in Section 3.3, any entity enjoying the *svabhāvic* mode of existence is not caused to exist by anything extrinsic to it; in other words, its existence is not ontologically dependent. Śaṅkara reasoned that anything not causally dependent on anything else for its existence (or continuation) must lack parts – otherwise it would be dependent for its existence on those parts (*Brahma Sūtra Bhāṣya*, 1.1.31). This is how he arrives at monism about the fundamental nature of ultimate reality. As Jessica Frazier has recently pointed out, Śaṅkara had additional reasons for defending monism. One of these was his conviction that a monist account of the nature of reality had more power to explain the way the world actually is than did rival ontologically pluralist theories (Frazier 2022).

Śaṅkara was well aware that this radical monist view has a host of further consequences. For one, lacking properties *nirguṇa Brahman* is outside the realm of possible experience. For another, because *nirguṇa Brahman* is a unity, we cannot talk or think about it, except conventionally. For this reason, he introduced *saguṇa Brahman* (*Brahman* with properties) into his system. *Saguṇa Brahman* is a personal creator God, who is an object of religious feeling and devotion. Śaṅkara's careful articulation of the relation between *nirguṇa* and *saguṇa Brahman* in his *Brahma Sūtra Bhāṣya* is one of the most creative features of his philosophical system. Essentially, in keeping with his commitment to monism, he holds that *saguṇa Brahman* is *nirguṇa Brahman*. The former is how the latter appears when projected (Śaṅkara's word is *adhyāsa*, which is often translated into English as 'superimposition') by consciousness into the conventional world of our experience. Śaṅkara held superimposition to be ubiquitous. He describes 'a beginningless and endless natural process of superimposition, whose nature is misconception, which creates agents and experiencers, and is directly known to everybody' (*Brahma Sūtra Bhāṣya*, 1.1.1, translated in Bartley (2011: 143)).

Śaṅkara's view is interesting for many reasons. His struggle to explain the relation between the ultimate and the conventional realm provides an instructive comparison to the ways in which this issue was dealt with by religious philosophers in non-Asian traditions (Clooney 1993). The language used and the conceptual framework may be different, but the relationship between transcendence and immanence, God *an sich* and God as he might enter into human experience, has been at the heart of Western theology and religious philosophy since the earliest times (see Martin Ganeri (2015b) for a discussion of Vedānta and Western theism). Moreover, considering Śaṅkara's view in relation to the Buddhist theories examined in this Element brings into relief the most significant philosophical commitments of both traditions, as well as their perceived consequences.

Śaṅkara's view also has contemporary relevance for the philosophy of religion, because many of the issues he grappled with have not gone away. Examining how he handled the philosophical problems raised by his radically monist metaphysics and epistemology might show roads not taken in analogous Western discussions about the nature of ultimate reality and our possibilities of coming to know it. Moreover, it is rarely noticed that Śaṅkara's actual influence on current philosophy of religion has been profound. His characterization of *nirguṇa Brahman* was a key influence on John Hick's theory of religious pluralism, which attempted to explain religious diversity by positing a qualityless and inaccessible Real underlying all religions (Barua 2015).

Many of the philosophical questions discussed in this section have proven to be of perennial interest. The answers given to them are, moreover, still contributing to exciting and innovative philosophical work (see Priest (2014) for one example). As we shall see, the same can be said of the material covered in the following section, which concerns how early Chinese philosophers dealt with questions about being and becoming.

4 Nothing and Something

The philosophical traditions of classical China are often regarded as predominantly concerned with ethical, social, and political issues. This emphasis can make them seem remote from the metaphysical, epistemological, and religious concerns of the Indian traditions. Closer inspection of the Chinese material, however, reveals a rich stratum of philosophical speculation on the nature of existence and the origins of being. This metaphysical interest is especially noticeable in the ancient divinatory manual, the *Yijing* (Wilhelm & Baynes 1977), and in the foundational text of philosophical Daoism, the *Daodejing* (Lau 1963).[11]

Here we explore some of the metaphysical perspectives found in early Chinese traditions, paying particular attention to understandings of the relation between nothing (*wu* 無) and something (*you* 有), a relation that was often taken to be the key to understanding cosmic generation. The reader will notice that this Element does not employ the term 'nothingness'. As will become clear in Section 4.4, this is because 'nothingness' can suggest an ontological commitment in a way that the term 'nothing' does not. Given the importance of the notion, and the heavy philosophical weight it carries, it is preferable to use the more neutral term.

4.1 Outline

Section 4 introduces key texts, before focusing on the notions of nothing and something found in the *Daodejing* (Lau 1963). Two rival traditional interpretations of nothing and something are explained, each of which aligns with a different view of cosmic generation and impacts how human beings, and

[11] This Element follows the convention of using the terms 'Daoism', 'early Daoism', and 'Daoist' for convenience. These terms were coined retrospectively to refer to thinkers whose ideas could be associated with the *Daodejing* or the *Zhuangzi* (see Section 4.2). Some scholars refer to the 'Lao-Zhuang tradition' to avoid giving the erroneous impression that already in ancient times Daoism was a movement rather than a style of living and thinking practised by individuals.

their moral and spiritual constitution, are regarded. The section discusses the significance for both spirituality and aesthetics of holding nothing to be an ontologically foundational reality that can be conceptually represented as spatial. The section then explores a different perspective on nothing and something, according to which nothing is in fact something: it is the primordial state of the universe, prior to differentiation.

The section explains that Daoist perspectives on nothing and something provided the principal lens for the interpretation of Buddhist teaching within China. The connection between the notion of nothing in the Chinese thought world and that of *śūnyatā* in the domain of Indian thought is highlighted. The iterations of Buddhism that emerged in China were significant not only for the evolution of Chinese culture, but they also had a profound impact on later developments within Buddhism in India and Tibet, as well as on the philosophy of Advaita Vedānta (see Section 3.9). The Daoist perspectives on nothing and something that were transmitted through Buddhism were also eventually assimilated into Confucian philosophy, which underwent a creative transformation from the eighth to the eleventh century CE (Harrison 2019: 190–9).[12] The section concludes with a brief discussion of neo-Confucian philosophy, which was the mature fruit of the long intellectual exchange between the three main streams of philosophical and spiritual reflection in China, namely, Daoism, Buddhism, and Confucianism.

4.2 Texts

The three principal classical Chinese texts referred to in this section are the *Yijing* (易經), the *Daodejing* (道德經), and the *Zhuangzi* (莊子) (see Cleary (2003) for English translations). The *Yijing* is known in English as *The Book of Changes* and, in the older Wade Giles system for representing Chinese in Roman script, as the *I Ching*. Because of its antiquity and archaic language, this text is notoriously difficult to translate (Legge (1975) and Wilhelm and Baynes (1977) are two of the best attempts). The *Yijing*'s origins are obscure, and its form has changed significantly over time. It began in ancient times as a divinatory manual, and was used by the kings of the Western Zhou dynasty (this dynasty was established at around 1050 BCE). Despite its antiquity and the peculiar nature of the text, the *Yijing* is still widely used today and is regarded as a classic of world literature (see Smith (2012) for a fascinating biography of the *Yijing*). The cosmological speculations within the *Yijing* provided the

[12] The full story of the interpenetration across various philosophical traditions of the ideas discussed in this section does not end with neo-Confucianism. In the nineteenth century, these ideas – as they were transmitted through neo-Confucianism – played a key role in the mature articulation of Sino-Muslim philosophy in the work of Ma Dexin (Petersen 2018: 70–9).

foundations for the philosophical and religious systems that developed in China long after its compilation (Liu 2006). Early Chinese thought on the cosmic principles of *yin* and *yang* is found in the *Yijing* (see Cheng (2009) and Wang (2012) on the significance of these). It also contains the first presentation of the system of trigrams and hexagrams that was to have a decisive impact on the Sinitic intellectual heritage (Wilhelm & Wilhelm 1979).

The *Daodejing* (*Tao Te Ching* in the older system of romanization) is probably the most well-known Chinese text outside China, like the *Yijing*, it is widely regarded as a world classic of religious literature. The *Daodejing* was formerly known as the *Laozi*, an eponymous title that reflects the traditional belief that the text was composed by the legendary Daoist sage Laozi (老子). While that belief is now usually dismissed by scholars outside China, it continues to be normal practice to refer to Laozi as if he were the author of the text rather than a legendary figure. This convention is useful because it allows scholars to avoid frequent repetition of the cumbersome phrase 'the unknown authors of the *Daodejing*'. In fact, it is obvious that the *Daodejing* is the work of multiple authors and editors as the text is composed of various strata and does not have a single narrative thread or authorial voice. Keeping this in mind makes it easier to recognize that the *Daodejing* does not promote a single philosophical perspective but contains a variety of thematically connected yet distinctive views. Despite considerable uncertainty about the origins of the material contained in the *Daodejing*, it is generally agreed that the compilation reached its final form sometime in the second century of the Common Era. There are now many good English translations of the *Daodejing*, for which D.C. Lau's translation sets the standard (Lau 1963). Some newer translations, such as that by Victor Mair (1990), rely on a slightly different version of the text, known as the Mawangdui version after the place in Hunan province of south-eastern China where, in an exciting archaeological discovery during the 1960s, textual fragments differing from the standard version of the text were found. This discovery demonstrated that variant readings of the *Daodejing* were still in circulation between 193 BCE and 140 BCE, when the tomb in which the fragments were discovered was sealed.

The *Zhuangzi* is another important classical text of philosophical Daoism. It is named after the philosopher and sage Zhuangzi (莊子), who is usually thought to have lived from 369 to 286 BCE. This text shows a clear thematic development from the *Yijing* and the *Daodejing* (Harrison 2019: Chapter 5), and, like them, it is not the product of a single author. Only chapters 1–7 are generally regarded as authentically representing Zhuangzi's thought, and these are referred to as the Inner Chapters. When dealing with texts as complex as the *Zhuangzi*, it is always advisable to consult more than one translation.

See Graham (2001) for a translation and commentary on the Inner Chapters of the *Zhuangzi* and see Ziporyn (2009) for an alternative translation.

The texts introduced in this section each gave rise to extensive commentarial traditions that continued for many centuries after the texts reached their final forms. In China, as in India, during the Common Era, commentarial traditions were the principal medium through which philosophical ideas and insights were transmitted to successive generations. Those who wrote commentaries on ancient texts were not, however, merely explaining the ideas of others but often propagated novel theories and ideas of their own. This process was assisted, indeed necessitated, by the concise character of many of the ancient texts (this is especially true of the *Yijing*). The commentarial tradition was particularly productive in China during the Wei-Jin period of neo-Daoism in the third century CE. Section 4.4 introduces two rival interpretations of a key chapter of the *Daodejing* that were advanced within this neo-Daoist commentarial tradition.

4.3 Nothing and Cosmology in the *Daodejing*

The content of the *Daodejing* is highly speculative. In its characteristic poetic style, it addresses a wide range of deep and perplexing philosophical questions. One of these questions concerns how to properly conceive of the notion of nothing (*wu* 無) in relation to the origin and constitution of the material things (*you* 有) that populate the cosmos. This question is the focus of Section 4.4. A related question concerns how, if at all, we might encounter 'nothing'. This second question is the focus of Section 4.9. The *Daodejing* addresses both of these questions in the context of a background concern to shed light on the origin of the cosmos.

The *Daodejing* deals with these questions in several of its chapters, especially in its eleventh chapter, which Douglas Berger aptly describes as 'evocative', 'mysterious', and 'suggestive' (Berger 2014: 166). Because of these characteristics of chapter 11, and many other chapters, readers should not expect to find clear answers within the *Daodejing* to the questions with which it grapples. In fact, as we see in Section 4.4, two contrasting interpretations of the *Daodejing*'s answers to these questions about 'nothing' were in circulation during the third century of the Common Era.

4.4 Two Interpretations of Nothing and Something in the *Daodejing*

Both interpretations of the relationship between nothing (*wu* 無) and something (*you* 有) that are explained in this section result from attempts to draw out the meaning of Chapter 11 of the *Daodejing*, which, despite the hermeneutical challenges it poses, consists of only forty-nine Chinese characters (see Berger (2014) for a more detailed discussion of these two traditional interpretations and the philosophical questions they raise). As we shall see, the interpretation that won out in this third-century hermeneutical disagreement had a significant impact on what came to be regarded as the mainstream Daoist view of being and becoming.

According to the highly influential commentator Wang Bi (226–249 CE), 'nothing' refers to the emptiness within things, such as cups and rooms, without which these things would not exist for people to use. He took this to imply that the *Daodejing* teaches that nothing is the fundamental ontological reality required for anything to come into existence.[13]

Douglas Berger has provided an English translation of Chapter 11 of the *Daodejing* that aligns well with Wang Bi's ontological interpretation of nothing:

> Thirty spokes join at a hub;
> In its nothing (*wu* 無), there is (*you* 有) the use of the cart.
> Mixing clay produces a vessel;
> In its nothing (*wu* 無), there is (*you* 有) the use of the vessel.
> Cutting doors and windows produces a room;
> In its nothing (*wu* 無), there is (*you* 有) the use of the room.
> Thus, its something (*you* 有) produces benefit.
> Its nothing (*wu* 無) produces use. (Berger 2014: 167)

The rival interpretation, propounded by Zhong Hui (225–264 CE), resists the view that nothing is the singular ontologically foundational reality; holding instead that nothing (*wu* 無) and something (*you* 有) are on a par because both are required to constitute the objects that we encounter experientially, such as cups and rooms. According to Zhong Hui, while we might be able to separate analytically the nothing and the something that constitute any object, they must nonetheless form an irreducible unity for that object to exist at all. Furthermore, on this interpretation of the teaching of Chapter 11 of the *Daodejing*, nothing does not enjoy any ontological status at all apart from that which it has in relation to something (and vice versa).

Zhong Hui's interpretation is supported by the following translation of Chapter 11, which is provided by Berger:

13 We can compare Wang Bi's ontologizing of nothing to the tendency, noted in Section 3.8, of some Yogācāra philosophers to give an ontological interpretation of emptiness.

> Thirty spokes join at a hub;
> In its nothing (*wu*) and something (*you*) is the use of the cart.
> Mixing clay produces a vessel;
> In its nothing and something is the use of the vessel.
> Cutting doors and windows produces a room;
> In its nothing and something is the use of the room.
> Thus, its something produces benefit.
> Its nothing produces use. (Berger 2014: 168)

Berger points out that both translations of Chapter 11 are plausible renderings of the Chinese characters that form the original text and that the difference between them is largely the result of parsing. If close analysis of Chapter 11 is unable to adjudicate between the two interpretations, there would seem to be no way to judge on internal textual grounds which is closer to the original intention of the teaching recorded in the *Daodejing*. Fortunately, given the importance of the issues, two strategies are available to us. One strategy, which we pursue in Section 4.9, is to ask which interpretation coheres best with what we can reconstruct of the ancient thought world that we can glimpse in the *Yijing*, for this would have provided the intellectual context of early readers of the *Daodejing*. Another strategy is to consider which interpretation is more consonant with other chapters of the *Daodejing*, particularly those that concern the central concept of *Dao* (道).

4.5 Dao

Debate about the *Daodejing*'s teaching on the relation between nothing and something in everyday objects was connected to a wider hermeneutical question about its first chapter, which concerns the relationship between nothing and the origin of the cosmos:

> A way [*Dao*] can be a guide, but not a fixed path;
> names can be given, but not permanent labels.
> Nonbeing is called the beginning of heaven and earth;
> being is called the mother of all things.
> Always be passionless, thereby observe the subtle;
> ever intent, thereby observe the apparent.
> These two come from the same source but differ in name;
> both are considered mysteries.
> The mystery of mysteries
> is the gateway of marvels. (Cleary 2003: 11)

The standard interpretation of this chapter emphasizes the line 'Nonbeing is called the beginning of heaven and earth', concluding that all things came from nothing, which aligns with Wang Bi's interpretation of Chapter 11. Likewise,

Chapter 40 highlights this same set of ideas: 'the ten thousand things are generated from what is (*you* 有), and what is (*you* 有) is generated from what is not (*wu* 無)' – 'the ten thousand things' being the stock expression used by classical Chinese authors to stand for 'everything that exists'.

The idea that all that is (*you* 有) is generated from nothing does not cohere well, however, with Chapter 4 of the *Daodejing*. There we find the claim that all things take form from the inexhaustible source of the *Dao*, which is itself formless and shapeless. Chapter 39, moreover, claims that all numbers as well as all things originate in the *Dao*, and that *Dao* is 'one'. Chapter 42 goes even further down this line of reflection by claiming that *Dao* generates oneness, from which eventually follows the ten thousand things. As Berger observes, 'during the third century, the question of how to grasp the relationship between *wu* and *you* was placed within the framework of the purported relationship between *wu* and *Dao* 道, understood as the "course" or "path" of the world's unfolding' (Berger 2014: 167).

Despite the lack of a consistent account of the relationship between nothing, something, and *Dao* across key chapters of the *Daodejing*, the idea that *Dao* could be identified with nothing dovetailed neatly with Wang Bi's interpretation of Chapter 11, and together these came to form the dominant reading of the text. As a result, the account of Daoist cosmology that came to be widely accepted from the third century CE held nothing to be both ontologically foundational and an ongoing essential constituent of everything that comes to be. In other words, nothing – understood as the formless, shapeless *Dao* – was regarded as both the original source of all beings and as that which sustains all things (*you* 有), including ourselves, in being. One implication of the claim that the cosmos-generating nothing is an essential constituent of all beings is that the nothing that originally gave rise to 'the ten thousand things' must be permanently intrinsic to them. Thus, the mainstream Daoist ontological perspective settled into the view that things are constituted by a particular relation of 'originary', primordial nothing and something (*you* 有), where 'something' amounts to the material form of that which exists (Berger 2014: 171).

4.6 Encountering Nothing

The two rival interpretations of Chapter 11 of the *Daodejing* that were explained in Section 4.4 hold different views about whether or not nothing (*wu* 無) has a more fundamental ontological status than something (*you* 有). Proponents of both interpretations nonetheless concur that nothing is a ubiquitous characteristic of all that we experience. The implication of this view was taken by subsequent Daoists to be that in experiencing something we are simultaneously encountering nothing. The message was that nothing, and thereby *Dao*, the ultimate mystery at the origin of all being, could be encountered in the most mundane objects of our experience. This is an extraordinary convergence, in another cultural register, with the Mādhyamikas' conviction that the objects of our experience are empty (see Section 3.5). It is remarkable that, in the early centuries of the Common Era, philosophers in both China and India were grappling with the fundamental ontological question of how nothing/emptiness and something/form come into relation to constitute both the world that we experience and ourselves as the experiencers of that world.

4.7 Nothing as Spatial

In its attempt to say something intellectually graspable about nothing, the *Daodejing* deploys the device of linking the notion of nothing to that of empty space. For example, in Chapter 11, nothing (*wu* 無) is explicated in terms of the emptiness between walls that makes a physical structure into a room. In addition to highlighting that it is the space within objects, such as rooms and cups, that makes them what they are, Chapter 11 points out that the space within objects also makes our use of them possible (see Section 4.4). The representation of nothing (*wu* 無) as spatial is, arguably, the most distinctive feature of the philosophical account of the relation between nothing and something found within and inspired by the *Daodejing*.

The explication of nothing in terms of empty space found in the *Daodejing* opened new dimensions of the philosophical investigation into being and becoming. The conceptual connection between nothing and empty space became one of the foundational assumptions for many different approaches both to cosmology and to spiritual practice within East Asia. It quickly led, for instance, to the high valuation of empty spaces (*kong* 空) that eventually, after the passage of many centuries, inspired the remarkable, austere aesthetic tradition of Zen Buddhism. This development within Zen no doubt also built on the connection between space and meditation made in several verses within the Pāli Canon, for example:

> Rāhula, develop meditation that is like space; for when you develop meditation that is like space, arisen agreeable and disagreeable contacts will not invade your mind and remain. Just as space is not established anywhere, so too, Rāhula, develop meditation that is like space; for when you develop meditation that is like space, arisen agreeable and disagreeable contacts will not invade your mind and remain. (*Mahārāhulovāda Sutta*, in Ñāṇamolí and Bodhi (2001: 530))

> 'Bhikkhus, suppose a man came with crimson, turmeric, indigo, or carmine and said: "I shall draw pictures and make pictures appear on empty space."

> What do you think, bhikkhus? Could that man draw pictures and make pictures appear on empty space?' – 'No, venerable sir. Why is that? Because empty space is formless and non-manifestive; it is not easy to draw pictures there or make pictures appear there . . . . Eventually the man would reap only weariness and disappointment.'
>
> 'So too, bhikkhus, there are these five courses of speech ... Herein, bhikkhus, you should train thus: "Our minds will remain unaffected ... and starting with him, we shall abide pervading the all-encompassing world with a mind similar to empty space, abundant, exalted, immeasurable, without hostility and without ill will." That is how you should train, bhikkhus.' (*Kakacūpama Sutta*, in Ñāṇamolí and Bodhi (2001: 221–2))

Within Daoism the initial conceptual connection between nothing and empty space paved the way for the Daoist philosopher, Zhuangzi (see Section 4.2), to regard the skilled use of space as a spiritual art (see Slingerland (2003) for discussions of this theme, and see Chapter 2 of the *Zhuangzi* for an example). Zhuangzi also established the trend, which was to become entrenched with later Daoism, of regarding sages as characterized by their embodiment of nothing (Chan 2014). Such a state was held to be marked by a general stance of being unperturbed and a lack of emotional response to the vicissitude of life and death.

As noted in Section 4.4, the neo-Daoist commentator on the *Daodejing*, Wang Bi, emphasized that empty space makes possible the material configurations that result in the existence of objects. This idea developed into the view that objects are constituted by material parts held together by their relations within space, with space being seen as the grounding and foundational reality holding composite objects together and making them what they are. Imagine, for a moment, a world not populated by physical objects, such as desks and chairs, plants and animals, but instead featuring a limitless expanse of empty space within which clusters of matter are suspended in configurations that sometimes make them useful for us. From such a perspective, space is not only ubiquitous but is also a unified and foundational reality.

The Chinese character that was used in the early Daoist commentarial tradition to refer to empty space was 空 (*kong*). This character is still commonly used in modern Chinese to refer to air, sky, empty space, and even free time. In both its ancient and modern usage, it also carries the connotations of expansiveness, limitlessness, and infinity. These connotations all reinforce the various conceptual connections that have been described in this section between originary nothing, emptiness, and *Dao*. As we saw in Section 4.6, the *Daodejing* moved seamlessly from reflection on empty spaces in humble everyday objects, like houses and cups, to speculation about the origin of the cosmos and the generation of 'the ten thousand things' (see Section 4.5).

4.8 Nothing and *Śūnyatā*

The affinity between the Daoist notion of empty space (*kong* 空) and the Indian Buddhist notion of *śūnyatā* (emptiness) did not go unnoticed by the early interpreters of Buddhism within China. During the first few centuries of the Common Era, Buddhism gradually spread across China. By the time it was sufficiently well established to have enough of a literate Chinese following to require the translation of Sanskrit sūtras into Chinese, Daoist reflections on nothing (*wu* 無) and empty space (*kong* 空) were already highly evolved. It was natural, then, for Chinese translators of Indian Buddhist sūtras to render the Sanskrit term *śūnyatā* (emptiness) as *kong* 空. In the Indian sūtras, however, the notion of *śūnyatā* always remained conceptually connected to the denial that any entity enjoyed the *svabhāvic* mode of existence (see Section 3.3). This conceptual connection was completely absent from the Chinese translations of these sūtras, which instead suggested that empty space (*kong* 空) was the foundational grounding reality within which material objects were somehow suspended.

The next bold philosophical move connected this Chinese Buddhist understanding of emptiness with the stream of Yogācāra philosophy which held that the objects of consciousness are internal to consciousness (see Section 3.8). *Kong* 空 thus came to be associated with consciousness, and consciousness in turn came to be regarded as the 'space' within which all 'things' come into being and continue in being. This set of associations was highly influential on Buddhist philosophy as it developed in both Japan (Kopf 2014) and Korea (Kim 2014). The influence of these ideas also extended into modern philosophy through the Kyoto school (*Kyōto-gakuha*), which was the most important school of philosophy in Japan during the twentieth century. Philosophers within this school, such as Keiji Nishitani (1900–1990), continued to work with the web of meanings that was generated when the notion of *kong* 空 was used to interpret the Indian Buddhist technical term *śūnyatā* (Nishitani 1982). The Kyoto school is also notable because it brought this traditional Asian perspective on nothing/emptiness into creative interaction with key themes and ideas from modern Western philosophy, particularly drawing on the two seminal German philosophers, Immanuel Kant (1724–1804) and Martin Heidegger (1889–1976). Philosophers in the Kyoto school deployed traditional perspectives on emptiness to address what they regarded as the most serious philosophical problem of their times, namely, how to respond to nihilism (see Davis (2019) for an introduction to the Kyoto school).

All the striking philosophical developments reviewed in this section, and in Section 4.6, in one way or another, were extrapolations of Wang Bi's understanding of the notion of nothing (*wu* 無). As we have seen, Wang took nothing to be the foundational ontological reality from which all beings were generated. This view, combined with the identification of *Dao* with nothing, proved more popular than Zhong Hui's alternative view, which accorded nothing a less elaborate ontological role. As noted earlier, Wang's position became the dominant interpretation of the *Daodejing*'s teaching, and it is still taken for granted by many people today. As we shall see in the next section, however, it has recently been suggested that Wang's interpretation was flawed by his failure to acknowledge both a crucial ambiguity in the *Daodejing*'s references to nothing and the background cosmological understanding that would have been taken for granted in its original context.

4.9 The Meaning of 'Nothing'

The account of Daoist cosmology introduced earlier in this section presents early Daoists as holding that being emerges from originary, primordial nothing. JeeLoo Liu has recently challenged this understanding, claiming instead that early Daoists never held there to be a state of primordial absolute nothingness (Liu 2014). Liu argues that the ontological conception of nothing, which supported the view that being emerges from nothing, was the result of Wang Bi's failure to acknowledge a significant ambiguity in the *Daodejing*'s notion of nothing. According to Liu, the two most important possible meanings of 'nothing' in circulation at the time of the *Daodejing*'s compilation were (i) 'what seems to be nothing but is actually something' and (ii) 'the original void' (Liu 2014: 182). Liu points out that Wang Bi concentrated on the second of these meanings rather than the first, and she notes that the first meaning is more consistent with the ancient cosmological speculations found in the *Yijing*, which early Daoists would have taken for granted.

Liu's argument is significant because, if it is correct, the common identification of *Dao* with nothing or non-being is unfaithful to the classical Daoist perspective. Liu cites Chapter 25 of the *Daodejing* as textual evidence that, prior to the third-century CE interpretations of the neo-Daoists, *Dao* was regarded as something rather than nothing: 'There is *something* (*youwu* 有物) undifferentiated and yet complete, which existed before heaven and earth' (Liu 2014: 183). Liu notes that Chapter 21 of the *Daodejing* also supports this reading:

> The *thing* [物 *wu*, thing] that is called *Dao* is eluding and vague. Vague and eluding, there is in it the form. Eluding and vague, in it are things. Deep and obscure, in it is the essence. The essence is very real; in it are evidences (*sic.*). (Here Liu relies on Chan's translation, Chan (1973: 150))

The main point of this exegetical argument is to invite us to re-evaluate, what Liu regards as, the overly metaphysical and spiritualized conception of *Dao* so that we might regain an understanding that is closer to the original one. To reach back to the earlier understanding of *Dao* requires a closer look into the cosmological speculations of the *Yijing*, which can be regarded as the foundational text of Chinese civilization. Until Liu's ground-breaking work, one of the great puzzles in the history of Chinese philosophy was how to explain the connection between the *Yijing* and the later Daoist classics the *Daodejing* and the *Zhuangzi*. According to Liu, the key to this lies in a shared cosmology.

4.10 The *Yijing*, *Dao*, and the Primordial State

The idea that being emerges out of nothing found in the *Daodejing*, as we have seen in Section 4.9, may not imply that early Daoists held being literally to come from nothing. This is because, according to the earliest Daoist understanding that we can reconstruct, 'nothing' may in fact be something. Following Liu's argument, the *Daodejing* implicitly relies on an ancient cosmological framework, found in the *Yijing*, in which the original state of the universe was thought to be formless rather than nothing. Liu notes that this cosmological framework is explicit in the *Zhuangzi*, where 'the initial, pre-ordered state of the universe is a state of "chaos (*hundun*)"' (Liu 2014: 184).

The central concept in this cosmological framework is *qi* (a term that is untranslatable into English but can roughly be rendered as 'vital force' or 'energy'). Liu claims that we will fail to understand the early Daoist perspective on *wu* 無 and *Dao* unless we consider its conceptual framing within *qi*-cosmology (Liu 2014: 183). Taking this framing into account, Liu suggests that the notion of *Dao* found in the *Daodejing* is derived from a 'conception of *qi* in its initial state' and that the notion of *Dao* 'could be an idealized conception of the nature and operation of *qi*' (Liu 2014: 183). Liu argues persuasively that this interpretation allows us to make better sense of the connection between the *Daodejing* and the *Yijing* than the alternative interpretation which overlooks *qi*-cosmology and ontologizes nothing. She also notes that the interpretation of *Dao* in terms of *qi*-cosmology is consistent with those parts of the *Daodejing* that were difficult to reconcile with the view that being emerges from primordial nothing. One such passage is Chapter 42 of the *Daodejing*: 'Everything carries *yin* and embraces *yang*. *Qi's* mutual agitation constitutes harmony' (Liu 2014: 183). *Qi*, then, is the formless primordial state from which all being emerges. Liu explains further that 'the *Daodejing*'s cosmological claim is that, in the beginning, there was *qi* in its primordial state, and this formless primordial *qi* is what the *Daodejing* refers to as "nothing (*wu*, 無)" when it says that something is generated by nothing' (Liu 2014: 183). On this reading, *Dao* can be understood not as an abstract metaphysical entity but more as a living thing constituted by *qi*.

4.11 The Supreme Ultimate

Despite the new perspective, briefly explained in Sections 4.9 and 4.10, which attempts to provide a historically accurate account of the meaning of the ancient Chinese texts, it remains the case that key concepts, such as *wu* 無 and *Dao* 道, have been interpreted in ways that tend towards metaphysics rather than naturalism. The more metaphysical interpretation that came to prominence in the commentarial tradition of the third century CE again came to the fore in the neo-Confucian philosophy that emerged in China, under the influence of Buddhism, from the eighth century CE.

By the eleventh century, two main schools of neo-Confucian philosophy had developed, the School of Laws or Principles and the School of Heart-Mind (for a concise account of these schools see Harrison (2019: 190–9); Liu (2018) provides a more detailed account). At the core of both schools was a theory about the evolution of the cosmos from an original unity. According to the School of Laws or Principles, the unity of the cosmos was grounded in a single underlying principle that united all individual things into the whole. This uniting principle came to be known as the supreme ultimate. One thinker from this school, Zhu Xi (1130–1200 CE), characterized the supreme ultimate as the 'highest of all, beyond which nothing can be. It is the most high, most mystical, and most abstruse, surpassing everything' (Fung 1976: 297). He adds that: 'With regard to heaven and earth in general, the Supreme Ultimate is in heaven and earth. And with regard to the myriad things in particular, the Supreme Ultimate is in every one of them too' (Fung 1976: 297).

To preserve the unity of the supreme ultimate, Zhu Xi concluded that it must be within all things in its entirety. This implied that the supreme ultimate in its entirety is within each human being, an idea which is key to neo-Confucian spirituality with its focus on transcending self-boundaries rather than on an idea of transcendence abstracted from the personal domain (Patt-Shamir 2021: 18). The figure of the sage thus came to be regarded as the human manifestation of the supreme ultimate. This initiated a debate about how those who were not yet sages could come to know the supreme ultimate that was already within them, with the rival views being either through introspection (an epistemological approach indebted to Zhuangzi) or through the more traditional methods of studying the classics and practising the rites. The School of Heart-Mind advocated the former approach, while the School of Laws or Principles advocated the latter.

4.12 Universal Mind

The neo-Confucian School of Heart-Mind reached its most sophisticated expression in the work of Wang Yangming (1472–1529 CE). Wang added to the idea of the unity of all things the conviction that, ultimately, the unity consists in a perfect correspondence between the mind and the world. This position is poised delicately between the two poles of idealism (which holds the mind to be ontologically foundational) and materialism (which regards matter as ontologically prior to mind). As P.J. Ivanhoe has argued, in Wang's conception, heart-mind and world are not external to one another but form a unity in which neither can be reduced to the other or eliminated (Ivanhoe 2009: 101–5).

Philosophers of the School of Heart-Mind posited an Original Heart-Mind to explain the unity of apparently individual heart-minds. Wang declared:

> The mind of man is Heaven. There is nothing that is not included in the mind of man. All of us are this single Heaven, but because of the obscurings caused by selfishness, the original state of heaven is not made manifest. Every time we extend our intuitive knowledge, we clear away the obscurings, and when all of them are cleared away, our original nature is restored, and we again become part of this Heaven. The intuitive knowledge of the part is the intuitive knowledge of the whole. The intuitive knowledge of the whole is the intuitive knowledge of the part. Everything is the single whole. (Fung 1976: 315)

The neo-Confucian theory of an original universal mind was the culmination of a long process of intellectual syncretism and cross-fertilization between various forms of Indian Buddhism, Daoism, Chinese Buddhism, and earlier Confucian thought (see Makeham (2018) for a study of Zhu Xi's assimilation of Buddhist thought). As such, despite its conclusion that everything making up the universe can be regarded as forming a unity, neo-Confucianism serves as a reminder that intellectual traditions do not stand alone but are the result of streams of influence flowing back as far as we are able to trace them. In the following section, we return to Indian thought and examine an ancient tradition whose core idea was that – whatever the universe is actually like – human beings will come to understand it through different perspectives.

5 Pluralism

This section introduces some key ideas from Jainism. The term 'Jain' is derived from the Sanskrit *ji*, which means to conquer or overcome. People adhering to this tradition are known as Jains, overcomers.[14] The Jain tradition still has

[14] 'Jains' is an anglicized pluralization. The term 'Jaina' transliterates the Sanskrit spelling, whereas 'Jain' transliterates the modern Indian pronunciation in languages such as Hindi and Kannada. This Element renders the singular 'Jain' and the plural 'Jains'.

a significant following within India, and it has, of course, evolved significantly over time. Its root is identifiable in the earliest strata of intellectual history within the Indian subcontinent. Like Buddhists, Jains reject the authority of the Vedas (see Section 2.3) and so constitute one of the main non-Brahmanical traditions of India. Their ethical code is distinctive for its rigorous commitment to non-violence towards all living beings, including plants.

Jains have always been important participants in Sanskrit intellectual culture, and they were involved in many of the key philosophical debates that have been discussed in this Element. Nonetheless, outside India, Jain philosophical positions are still not yet as familiar as those of the Buddhist schools. Jains advanced perspectival pluralism, which is a form of epistemological pluralism (see Section 5.4). Pluralist theories in general and, specifically, epistemological pluralism have been major concerns within twentieth- and twenty-first-century Western philosophy. Consequently, Jain philosophy is slowly gaining wider recognition as scholars investigate its distinctive ontological and epistemological positions (see Priest (2018) and Ganeri (2019) for examples).

5.1 Outline

This short section provides a concise introduction to Jain philosophy, outlining its origins and its foundational textual tradition. The section focuses on those aspects of Jain teaching which are most distinctive in the domains of ontology and epistemology, namely, perspectival pluralism, the theory of the many-sidedness of reality, the theory of the seven modes of assertion, and the pursuit of omniscience (see Jaini (1979) for a more general account of Jain teachings).

5.2 Origins

Māhavīra (c. 599–527 BCE) is traditionally regarded as the founder of Jainism. Many of Jainism's core ideas, such as the idea that consciousness is indestructible, were, however, in circulation long before Māhavīra's lifetime. It is not implausible to claim that Jain ideas reflect an archaic tradition that was widespread on the Indian subcontinent prior to the ascendancy of the Vedic tradition. Despite the difficulty of providing material evidence to support such speculation, many agree that the Jain tradition preserves a heritage of greater antiquity than that found in the teachings of the other philosophical traditions that flourished in the post-Vedic period (see McEvilley (2002) for a discussion).

5.3 Texts

The official Jain Canon of sacred texts was established at a council in the fifth century CE, although Jain teaching is based on an oral tradition that was first codified in the fourth century BCE. The foundational Jain sacred texts are available online, translated into English by Hermann Jacobi.[15] The first surviving systematic presentation of early Jain teaching, however, is found in the *Tattvārtha-sūtra*. This was composed in Sanskrit in the early centuries of the Common Era and is attributed to Umāsvāti (see Tatia (1994) for a modern English translation). The *Tattvārtha-sūtra* deals with a wide range of topics and, being the first extant text to elucidate early Jain logic, epistemology, and ontology, it is especially important to philosophers. Also of especial relevance to philosophers are the three treatises *Nyāyāvatāra*, *Nyāyāvatāra-vivṛti*, and *Nyāyāvatāra-ṭippana*, which concern developments of Jain logic and epistemology (Balcerowicz (2001) provides an English translation).

5.4 Perspectival Pluralism

Jain epistemology was shaped by the conviction that no entity possesses a unique essence that would allow it to be fully known through a single epistemic perspective (the Sanskrit term for 'perspective' is *naya*). The Jain account of the many-sidedness of reality is the result of this conviction about ontology. Because they took reality to be many-sided, Jains held that any philosophical theory would be inadequate to our epistemic needs unless it explicitly accommodated a plurality of perspectives. Philosophical theories, according to Jains, usually rely on a single epistemic perspective through which philosophers erroneously seek to understand a reality that is complex because it is many-sided. According to this view, disagreements between philosophical theories arise when one theory employs an epistemic perspective focusing on a particular 'side' of reality (the impermanence of entities, for example) while another theory employs an epistemic perspective focusing on a different 'side' of reality (the permanence of identity through change, for example). The Jain analysis of such disagreements avers that the apparently rival theories both yield conclusions that are partly right and partly wrong, because each theory is based on only one limited epistemic perspective. Jains argued that a fuller account of the truth could only be obtained by taking the deliverances of multiple epistemic perspectives into account. This conviction led them to develop their own distinctive philosophical theory – perspectival pluralism – that, rather than being based on just another single epistemic perspective, aspired to embrace a number of epistemic perspectives simultaneously.

[15] Jacobi's English translation of the *Jaina Sūtras*: www.sacred-texts.com/jai/sbe22/index.htm. Jacobi's translation was first published in 1884; although some of the transliteration of Sanskrit into Roman script is now dated, the translation has retained its value.

The Jain theory of perspectival pluralism was not a cry of despair heralding a plunge into scepticism in the face of long-standing and seemingly intractable philosophical disagreements. Nor was perspectival pluralism a concession to relativism about truth and our knowledge of it, for it is compatible with the view that reality can genuinely be known, even though any single perspective can only disclose a piece of it. Jains held that taking multiple epistemic perspectives into account was a precondition for knowledge and not a temporary inconvenience. Their theory of perspectival pluralism was proposed as a method to reconcile at a higher level of abstraction the deliverances of single epistemic perspectives by bringing them within the scope of a unified theory that operated at a higher conceptual level.

The ambitious theory of perspectival pluralism required Jains to provide an explanation of how we can use language to communicate successfully, given that what we say about entities does not usually reflect multiple epistemic perspectives. Assertions such as 'the dog is wet', for instance, do not convey knowledge about the complex many-sided entity which is the dog. Jains developed a highly nuanced theory of language to complement their theory of perspectival pluralism. Their view was that epistemic perspectives were analysable into modes of assertion, of which they identified the following seven:

1. Asserting.
2. Denying.
3. Assert-denying.
4. Both asserting and denying.
5. Both asserting and assert-denying.
6. Both denying and assert-denying.
7. Asserting, denying and assert-denying.

Jains held that the most complete description available to us of any object would have to cover all seven modes of assertion. The basic problem with unmodulated assertions like 'the dog is wet', according to Jains, is that they are not specific enough. Such assertions need to be reframed using the seven modes of assertion after being disambiguated carefully across, what Jains termed, parameters. They held that the parameters of substance, time, place, and state should be considered when disambiguating assertions (although, they noted that not every parameter would be relevant to every assertion). This was in recognition of the fact that an assertion about an object might be true with respect to some set of parameters, a particular time and place, for instance, and false with respect to another set of parameters. The dog, for example, may have been wet on Tuesday by the river but not wet on Wednesday in the apartment. To disambiguate the assertion 'the dog is wet' would require consideration of all the relevant parameters. The disambiguated assertion might then be 'with respect to some place and time, the dog is wet'. Having disambiguated the assertion, one might then proceed to analyse it according to the seven modes. (For another simple example, see Harrison (2019: 55–7); for a more detailed account, see Ganeri (2001: 128–50).)

Jains deployed the ideas explained in this section to make the point that philosophical disagreements, such as those between Buddhists and Hindus, arose because the apparently conflicting positions were based on a limited grasp of reality. They held that the truth about reality could only be attained when many different perspectives were allowed to contribute to an understanding of the whole, and they took themselves to have provided a method by which such a comprehensive vision could be achieved. They thus cultivated an irenic atmosphere, which was surely important for the successful pursuit of a spiritual life, the final goal of which was to achieve liberation from the cycle of rebirth. In the Jain understanding, such liberation implied a state of perfection characterized by omniscience. This explains the tight connection between Jainism as a spiritual tradition and its technical philosophical concerns.

5.5 Omniscience

As we have seen in Section 5.4, the Jain theory of perspectival pluralism emphasizes the limitations of our epistemic perspectives, unless the truths they disclose can be incorporated into a comprehensive vision. The method of analysis provided by the seven modes of assertion was thought to allow a limited human consciousness to expand its understanding of reality by integrating seven epistemic perspectives. Also found within Jainism, however, is the conviction that the full truth about our many-sided reality exceeds the possible epistemic perspectives that could be adopted by a limited human consciousness. This is because, as Piotr Balcerowicz puts it,

> To know one thing means to know everything, inasmuch as everything is interrelated. To know one singular entity, one should be required to know both all its modes, including past and future, and its complex interrelatedness, that is, the relations in which it entered, enters, and will enter with other entities, but also relations which are precluded. Otherwise, our knowledge of the singular thing would be partial. (Balcerowicz 2017: 79)

In short, knowledge of reality in all its dimensions was thought to require omniscience. Siddhasena's *Nyāyāvatāra* (verse 29) explains: 'Since a thing has manifold character, it is comprehended (only) by the omniscient' (quoted in Priest (2018: 86)). This strand of Jain teaching holds that, in principle, a consciousness that was without limits could occupy all possible epistemic perspectives simultaneously. If it did so, its knowledge of reality would be complete. This is the Jain idea of omniscience (*kevala*). Achieving this state is held by Jains to be the most important spiritual goal because it is tantamount to a state of perfection. A consciousness in a *kevalic* state is thought to be a consciousness with no limitations. Moreover, because an unlimited consciousness could not be constrained by the range of perspectives available to an embodied being, it is held by Jains to no longer be the subject of rebirth.

We can speculate that this remarkable position developed from the conviction, which is present in the earliest strata of Jain teaching and probably dates to archaic times, that consciousness is indestructible. It is easy to see how combining this conviction with a belief in rebirth could lead to the view that a single consciousness would eventually have been embodied in every possible type of material life form and so would have occupied every possible epistemic perspective. An omniscient consciousness might originally have been regarded as one that had accumulated all possible perspectives and had thus acquired full knowledge of reality. We can conjecture how such an understanding of omniscience may have been gradually transformed into the account explained in the previous paragraph through its assimilation into a sophisticated philosophical system. Speculative as it is, this theory can account for the distinctive emphasis within Jainism on non-violence towards all life forms, even those, such as flies, to which other Indian traditions do not typically assign value.

Whatever the origins of the Jain understanding of omniscience may be, the philosophical debate about it was already underway at the time when both Jainism and Buddhism were gaining recognition as distinctive philosophical schools. During this time, the following account of Māhavīra's epistemic powers was in circulation:

> When the Venerable Ascetic Māhavīra had become a Jina and Arhat, he was a Kevalin, omniscient and comprehending all objects; he knew and saw all conditions of the world, of gods, of men, and demons; whence they come, wither they go, whether they are born as men or animals or become gods or hell-beings, the ideas, the thought of their minds, the food, doings, desires, the open and secret deeds of all living beings in the whole world; he the Arhat, for whom there is no secret, knew and saw all conditions of all living beings in the world, what they thought, spoke, or did at any moment. (Jacobi (1884: 263–4), transliteration slightly amended)

Accounts like this seem to have started something of an arms race in the ancient world – with rival groups of devotees making increasingly extravagant claims about their teachers. In the face of this extravagance, we can appreciate the more restricted form of epistemic pluralism that characterized Jain philosophy during the Common Era. As we have seen, in a move that facilitated the reconciliation of apparently rival philosophical views, Jains constrained a potentially infinite number of epistemic perspectives to those aligned with seven modes of assertion. Indeed, for this achievement Jains can be regarded as constituting a model of good practice for philosophical pluralism more generally. Such models are especially important in the twenty-first century as philosophy of religion, and philosophy more generally, becomes increasingly global.

6 Global Philosophy

Research focused on Asian philosophical traditions has increased dramatically over the past several decades. Foundational work in both Indian and Chinese traditions has made excellent translations of key texts widely accessible. Despite all that has been achieved so far, and the exponential rate at which new primary and secondary material becomes available, this remains a field of research in which new archaeological discoveries and hermeneutical insights can change seemingly well-established perspectives in unexpected ways. As Indian and Chinese traditions become increasingly familiar to many Western readers, research continues to expand on, for example, Korean philosophy (Ch'oe et al. 2000; Ivanhoe 2016), Japanese philosophy (Dilworth et al. 1998; De Bary et al. 2001; Ivanhoe 2016), and Tibetan philosophy (Kapstein 2001; Thakchöe 2007).

The wealth of accessible and reliable material now available in English and other European languages on Asian traditions converges with what has been, arguably, the most exciting development within academic philosophy of religion within recent decades. Namely, the trend towards expanding the subject area of the discipline to reach beyond its traditional focus on arguments and ideas connected to Western theism.[16] This trend is part of a creative research agenda which is now testing the boundaries of global philosophy (see Connolly (2015) for a discussion of some of the methodological issues raised by global philosophy). In surveying key topics and arguments within Asian philosophy of religion, some of which bear directly on concerns within current analytic philosophy of religion, this Element has highlighted philosophical issues of potentially global concern, such as the nature of the self, and how to conceptualize the relation between being and becoming. Significant recent work within the philosophy of religion, and within philosophy more broadly, has drawn on philosophical ideas and arguments from both the East and the West to advance

[16] For a discussion of this trend, see an online interview with the author: https://closertotruth.com/ctt-chats/victoria-harrison-philosophy-world-religions.

our understanding of these and other issues (see Priest (2014) for an example of this kind of philosophical work at its finest).

Asian traditions are also providing inspiration for the development of new philosophical theories. Jonardon Ganeri, for instance, has recently suggested that rather than focus exclusively on the technical details of the Jain theory of perspectival pluralism, we might take it as model for a form of epistemic pluralism that is not a pluralism of theories but a pluralism of epistemic stances or standpoints (Ganeri 2019). He proposes interpreting Jain epistemic perspectives as practical attitudes that guide inquiry by targeting attention to particular facets of reality, such as to what is present to experience. This creative interpretation portrays the *nayas* (perspectives) as strategies for generating belief that are dynamically responsive to different epistemic contexts. On this view, the *nayas* are more akin to what William Alston has, in another context, called 'belief-forming mechanisms' than they are to static conceptual vantage points from which the subject cannot move (Alston 1993). The Jain theory of perspectival pluralism is thus morphed into a pluralist account of belief-forming strategies, or, as Ganeri puts it, a plurality of 'action-guiding policies governing the application of epistemic principles' (Ganeri 2019: 7). As such, Jain philosophy gains a new relevance to issues of concern today.

In view of the growing body of work adopting a syncretic approach to ideas from different traditions, some current philosophers of religion have suggested jettisoning the distinction between Eastern and Western philosophy or, at least, reserving its use for work concerned with the history of philosophy (Harrison (2020), for instance). Such a move would encourage free deployment of the conceptual resources of a broad range of the world's philosophical traditions in response to the philosophical problems that are of concern in an increasingly globalized environment. Among these conceptual resources, the phenomenological tools honed by the Yogācāra philosophers, along with the Mādhyamikas' approach to ontology, seem particularly ripe to contribute to the global philosophical project, given its current focus on understanding the psychology of experience and cognition combined with a predilection for ontological parsimony.

This Element has expounded ideas and arguments largely in abstraction from the forms of life and traditions of spiritual practice they inform. The insights the Element contains are largely the result of the author's grounding in the methods of analytic philosophy and the Element's goal has been to provide a clear and concise scholarly introduction to Asian philosophy of religion. Nonetheless, the author is aware from her own experience that many of the ideas presented here can have extraordinary transformative power on the lives of those who engage with them. The analytic understanding of the issues presented here invites further elaboration by philosophers who are themselves immersed in the traditions of spiritual practice in which these ideas found their original home.

References

Alston, W. P. (1993). *Perceiving God: The Epistemology of Religious Experience*, Ithaca, NY: Cornell University Press.

Balcerowicz, P. (2001). *Jaina Epistemology in Historical and Comparative Perspective. Critical Edition and English Translation of Logical-Epistemological Treatises: Nyāyāvatāra, Nyāyāvatāra-vivṛti, and Nyāyāvatāra-ṭippana*, Stuttgart: Franz Steiner.

Balcerowicz, P. (2017). Jainism: Disambiguate the Ambiguous. In J. Tuske, ed., *Indian Epistemology and Metaphysics*. London: Bloomsbury Academic, pp. 75–100.

Baldwin, E. & McNabb, T. D. (2019). *Plantingian Religious Epistemology and World Religions: Prospects and Problems*, Lanham, MD: Lexington Books.

Bartley, C. (2011). *An Introduction to Indian Philosophy*, London: Continuum.

Barua, A. (2015). Hick and Radhakrishnan on Religious Diversity: Back to the Kantian Noumenon. *Sophia*, 54: 181–200. https://doi.org/10.1007/s11841-015-0459-z.

Berger, D. (2014). The Relation of Nothing and Something: Two Classical Chinese Readings of *Daodejing* 11. In J. Liu & D. Berger, eds., *Nothingness in Asian Philosophy*. London: Routledge, pp. 166–80.

Blumenthal, J. (2004). *The Ornament of the Middle Way: A Study of the Madhyamaka Thought of Śāntarakṣita*, Ithaca, NY: Snow Lion.

Bodhi, B. (2000). *The Connected Discourses of the Buddha: A Translation of the Saṃyutta Nikāya*, Boston, MA: Wisdom.

Brereton, J. P. (1990). The Upanishads. In W. T. DeBary & I. Bloom, eds., *Approaches to the Asian Classics*. New York: Columbia University Press, pp. 115–35.

Bronkhorst, J. (2007). *Greater Magadha: Studies in the Culture of Early India*, Leiden, MA: Brill.

Burley, M. (2016). *Rebirth and the Stream of Life: A Philosophical Study of Reincarnation, Karma and Ethics*, New York: Bloomsbury.

Burton, D. (2014). *Emptiness Appraised: A Critical Study of Nāgārjuna's Philosophy*, London: Routledge.

Carpenter, A. D. (2014). *Indian Buddhist Philosophy*, Durham: Acumen.

Chan, A. (2014). Embodying Nothingness and the Ideal of the Affectless Sage in Daoist Philosophy. In J. Liu & D. Berger, eds., *Nothingness in Asian Philosophy*. London: Routledge, pp. 213–29.

Chan, W.-t., ed. (1973). *A Sourcebook in Chinese Philosophy*, 4th ed., Princeton, NJ: Princeton University Press.

Cheng, C.-y. (2009). The *Yi-Jing* and *Yin-Yang* Way of Thinking. In B. Mou, ed., *History of Chinese Philosophy*, Routledge History of World Philosophies, volume 3. Oxford: Routledge, pp. 71–106.

Ch'oe, Y., Lee, P. H. & De Bary, W. T., eds. (2000). *Sources of Korean Tradition, volume 2: From the Sixteenth to the Twentieth Centuries*, New York: Columbia University Press.

Cleary, T., trans. (1993). *The Flower Ornament Scripture: A Translation of the Avatamsaka Sutra*, Boston, MA: Shambhala.

Cleary, T., trans. (1998). *The Sutra of Hui-neng: Grand Master of Zen*, Boston, MA: Shambhala.

Cleary, T. (2003). *The Taoist Classics: The Collected Translations of Thomas Cleary*, volume 1, Boston, MA: Shambhala.

Clooney, F. X. (1993). *Theology after Vedānta: An Experiment in Comparative Theology*, Delhi: Sri Satguru.

Connolly, T. (2015). *Doing Philosophy Comparatively*, London: Bloomsbury Academic.

Dasti, M. (2012). Asian Philosophy. In C. Taliaferro, V. S. Harrison & S. Goetz, eds., *The Routledge Companion to Theism*. London: Routledge, pp. 23–37.

Davis, B. W. (2019). The Kyoto School. In E. N. Zalta, ed., *The Stanford Encyclopedia of Philosophy*, Summer ed. https://plato.stanford.edu/archives/sum2019/entries/kyoto-school/.

De Bary, W. T., Keene, D., Tanabe, G., Varley. P., eds. (2001). *Sources of Japanese Tradition, volume 1: From Early Times to the Sixteenth Century*, New York: Columbia University Press.

Dilworth, D. A., Vigielmo, V. H. & Zavala, A. J., eds. and trans. (1998). *Sourcebook for Modern Japanese Philosophy: Selected Documents*, Westport, CT: Greenwood Press.

Edelglass, W. & Garfield, J. L., eds. (2009). *Buddhist Philosophy: Essential Readings*, New York: Oxford University Press.

Flood, G. (1996). *An Introduction to Hinduism*, Cambridge: Cambridge University Press.

Frazier, J. (2022). Monism in Indian Philosophy: The Coherence, Complexity, and Connectivity of Reality in Śaṃkara's Arguments for Brahman. *Religious Studies*. https://doi.org/10.1017/S0034412522000117.

Fung, Y.-l. (1976). *A Short History of Chinese Philosophy: A Systematic Account of Chinese Thought from Its Origin to the Present Day*, New York: The Free Press.

Ganeri, J. (2001). *Philosophy in Classical India: The Proper Work of Reason*, London: Routledge.

Ganeri, J. (2011). *The Lost Age of Reason: Philosophy in Early Modern India 1450–1700*, Oxford: Oxford University Press.

Ganeri, J. (2012). *The Self: Naturalism, Consciousness, & the First-Person Stance*, Oxford: Oxford University Press.

Ganeri, J. (2015a). Analytic Philosophy in Early Modern India. In E. N. Zalta, ed., *The Stanford Encyclopedia of Philosophy*, Summer ed. https://plato.stanford.edu/archives/sum2015/entries/early-modern-india/.

Ganeri, J., ed. (2017). *The Oxford Handbook of Indian Philosophy*, Oxford: Oxford University Press.

Ganeri, J. (2019). Epistemic Pluralism: From Systems to Stances. *Journal of the American Philosophical Association*, 4(1): 1–21. https://doi.org/10.1017/apa.2018.34.

Ganeri, M. (2015b). *Indian Thought and Western Theism: The Vedānta of Rāmānuja*, London: Routledge.

Garfield, J. L., trans. and commentary. (1995). *The Fundamental Wisdom of the Middle Way: Nāgārjuna's Mūlamadhyamakakārikā*, Oxford: Oxford University Press.

Garfield, J. L. (2014). Madhyamaka, Nihilism, and the Emptiness of Emptiness. In J. Liu & D. Berger, eds., *Nothingness in Asian Philosophy*. London: Routledge, pp. 44–63.

Garfield, J. L. (2015). *Engaging Buddhism: Why It Matters to Philosophy*, Oxford: Oxford University Press.

Gowans, C. W. (2003). *Philosophy of the Buddha*, London: Routledge.

Graham, A. C. (2001). *Chang-tzu: The Inner Chapters*, Indianapolis, IN: Hackett.

Halbfass, W. (1988). *India and Europe*, New York: State University of New York Press.

Hale, B. (2013). *Necessary Beings: An Essay on Ontology, Modality, & the Relations Between Them*, Oxford: Oxford University Press.

Hamilton, S. (2001). *Indian Philosophy: A Very Short Introduction*, Oxford: Oxford University Press.

Harrison, V. S. (2006). The Pragmatics of Defining Religion in a Multi-cultural World. *International Journal for Philosophy of Religion*, 59(3): 133–52. https://doi.org/10.1007/s11153-006-6961-z.

Harrison, V. S. (2019). *Eastern Philosophy: The Basics*, 2nd ed., London: Routledge.

Harrison, V. S. (2020). Global Philosophy of Religion(s). *Religious Studies*, 56(1): 20–31. https://doi.org/10.1017/S0034412519000647.

Harvey, P. (2000). *An Introduction to Buddhist Ethics*, Cambridge: Cambridge University Press.

Harvey, P. (2013). *An Introduction to Buddhism: Teachings, History, and Practices*, 2nd ed., Cambridge: Cambridge University Press.

Ivanhoe, P. J., trans. (2009). *Readings from the Lu-Wang School of Neo-Confucianism*, Indianapolis, IN: Hackett.

Ivanhoe, P. J. (2016). *Three Streams: Confucian Reflections on Learning & the Moral Heart-Mind in China, Korea, and Japan*, New York: Oxford University Press.

Ivanhoe, P. J., Flanagan, O. J., Harrison, V. S., Sarkissian, H. & Schwitzgebel, E., eds. (2018). *The Oneness Hypothesis: Beyond the Boundary of Self*, New York: Columbia University Press.

Jacobi, H., trans. (1884). *Jaina Sūtras, Part 1*, Sacred Books of the East, volume 22, Oxford: Clarendon Press. www.sacred-texts.com/jai/sbe22/index.htm.

Jaini, P. S. (1979). *The Jaina Path of Purification*, Berkeley, CA: University of California Press.

Jamison, S. W. & Brereton, J. P., trans. (2014). *The Rigveda: The Earliest Religious Poetry of India*, 3 volumes, Oxford: Oxford University Press.

Kapstein, M. T. (2001). *Reason's Traces: Identity and Interpretation in Indian and Tibetan Buddhist Thought*, Somerville, MA: Wisdom Books.

Kim, H. (2014). Nothingness in Korean Buddhism: The Struggle against Nihilism. In J. Liu & D. Berger, eds., *Nothingness in Asian Philosophy.* London: Routledge, pp. 230–45.

King, R. (1997). *Early Advaita Vedānta and Buddhism*, Delhi: Sri Satguru.

King, R. (1999). *Indian Philosophy: An Introduction to Hindu and Buddhist Thought*, Edinburgh: Edinburgh University Press.

Kopf, G. (2014). Zen, Philosophy, and Emptiness: Dōgen and the Deconstruction of Concepts. In J. Liu & D. Berger, eds., *Nothingness in Asian Philosophy.* London: Routledge, pp. 246–62.

Kuznetsova, I., Ganeri, J. & Ram-Prasad, C., eds. (2012). *Hindu and Buddhist Ideas in Dialogue: Self and No-Self*, Farnham: Ashgate.

Lau, D. C., trans. (1963). *Tao Te Ching*, New York: Penguin.

Lee, P. H. & De Bary, W. T., eds. (1997). *Sources of Korean Tradition, volume 1: From Early Times to the Sixteenth Century*, New York: Columbia University Press.

Leftow, B. (2022). *Anselm's Argument: Divine Necessity*, Oxford: Oxford University Press.

Legge, J., trans. (1975). *The I Ching*, 2nd ed., New York: Dover Books.

Liu, J. (2006). *An Introduction to Chinese Philosophy: From Ancient Philosophy to Chinese Buddhism*, Oxford: Blackwell.

Liu, J. (2014). Was There Something in Nothingness? The Debate on the Primordial State between Daoism and Neo-Confucianism. In J. Liu &

D. Berger, eds., *Nothingness in Asian Philosophy.* London: Routledge, pp. 181–96.

Liu, J. (2018). *Neo-Confucianism: Metaphysics, Mind, and Morality*, Malden, MA: Wiley-Blackwell.

Liu, J. & Berger, D., eds. (2014). *Nothingness in Asian Philosophy*, London: Routledge.

Mair, V. M., trans. (1990). *Tao Te Ching*, New York: Bantam Books.

Makeham, J., ed. (2018). *The Buddhist Roots of Zhu Xi's Philosophical Thought*, Oxford: Oxford University Press.

Matilal, B. K. (2002). On the Concept of Philosophy in India. In J. Ganeri, ed., *The Collected Essays of Bimal Krishna Matilal: Mind, Language and World.* New Delhi: Oxford University Press, pp. 353–69.

Mayeda, S., trans. (1992). *A Thousand Teachings: The Upadeśasāhasri of Śankara*, Albany, NY: State University of New York Press.

McEvilley, T. (2002). *The Shape of Ancient Thought: Comparative Studies in Greek and Indian Philosophies*, New York: Allworth Press.

McNabb, T. D. & Baldwin, E. (2022). *Classical Theism and Buddhism: Connecting Metaphysical and Ethical Systems*, London: Bloomsbury.

Miller, J. (2005). *Daoism: A Short Introduction*, Oxford: Oneworld.

Moeller, H.-G. (2004). *Daoism Explained: From the Dream of the Butterfly to the Fishnet Allegory*, Chicago, IL: Open Court.

Ñāṇamolí, B. & Bodhi, B., trans. (2001). *The Middle Length Discourses of the Buddha: A Translation of the Majjhíma Níkāya*, 2nd ed., Boston, MA: Wisdom.

Nicholson, A. J. (2010). *Unifying Hinduism: Philosophy and Identity in Indian Intellectual History*, New York: Columbia University Press.

Nishitani, K. (1982). *Religion and Nothingness*, J. Van Bragt, trans., Berkeley, CA: University of California Press.

Olivelle, P., trans. (2014). *The Early Upaniṣads: Annotated Text and Translation*, Oxford: Oxford University Press.

Patt-Shamir, G. (2021). *Persons Emerging: Three Neo-Confucian Perspectives on Transcending Self-Boundaries*, Albany, NY: State University of New York Press.

Petersen, K. (2018). *Interpreting Islam in China: Pilgrimage, Scripture, and Language in the Han Kitab*, New York: Oxford University Press.

Pine, R., trans. and commentary. (2005). *The Heart of Wisdom Sūtra, Prajñāpār-amitāhṛdaya*, Washington, DC: Shoemaker & Hoard.

Prabhavananda, S. & Isherwood, C., trans. (2002). *Bhagavad-gītā: The Song of God*, New York: Signet Classic.

Priest, G. (2002). *Beyond the Limits of Thought*, Oxford: Clarendon Press.

Priest, G. (2014). *One: Being an Investigation into the Unity of Reality and of its Parts, Including the Singular Object Which is Nothingness*, Oxford: Oxford University Press.

Priest, G. (2018). *The Fifth Corner of Four: An Essay on Buddhist Metaphysics and the Catuṣkoṭi*, Oxford: Oxford University Press.

Radhakrishnan, S. & Moore, C. A., eds. (1989). *A Sourcebook in Indian Philosophy*, Princeton, NJ: Princeton University Press.

Sankaracarya. (1965). *Brahma Sūtra Bhāṣya of Shankaracharya*, trans. S. Gambhirananda, Calcutta: Advaita Ashram. https://archive.org/details/brahma-sutra-bhasya-of-sankaracharya-swami-gambhirananda.

Schmidt-Leukel, P. (2006). *Understanding Buddhism*, Edinburgh: Dunedin Academic Press.

Shulman, E. (2014). *Rethinking the Buddha: Early Buddhist Philosophy as Meditative Perception*, New York: Cambridge University Press.

Siderits, M. (2004). *Personal Identity and Buddhist Philosophy*, Aldershot: Ashgate.

Siderits, M. (2007). *Buddhism as Philosophy: An Introduction*, Aldershot: Ashgate.

Siderits, M. (2017). Comparison or Confluence in Philosophy. In J. Ganeri, ed., *The Oxford Handbook of Indian Philosophy*. Oxford: Oxford University Press, pp. 75–90.

Slingerland, E. (2003). *Effortless Action: Wu-Wei as Conceptual Metaphor and Spiritual Ideal in Early China*, Oxford: Oxford University Press.

Smith, R. (2012). *The I Ching: A Biography*, Princeton, NJ: Princeton University Press.

Suthren Hirst, J. G. (2005). *Advaita Vedānta: A Way of Teaching*, Abingdon: RoutledgeCurzon.

Takeuchi, Y., ed. (1997). *Buddhist Spirituality I: Indian, Southeast Asian, Tibetan and Early Chinese*, New York: Crossroad.

Tatia, N., trans. (1994). *That Which Is: A Classic Jain Manual for Understanding the True Nature of Reality: A Translation of Umāsvāti's Tattvārtha-sūtra*, New Haven, CT: Yale University Press.

Taylor, R. (1990). *The Religious Dimensions of Confucianism*, Albany, NY: State University of New York Press.

Thakchöe, S. (2007). *The Two Truths Debate: Tsongkhapa and Gorampa on the Middle Way*, Boston, MA: Wisdom.

Vetter, T. (1988). *The Ideas and Meditative Practices of Early Buddhism*, Leiden: Brill.

Walshe, M., trans. (1995). *The Long Discourses of the Buddha: A Translation of the Dīgha Níkāya*, Somerville, MA: Wisdom.

Wang, R. R. (2012). *Yingyang: The Way of Heaven and Earth in Chinese Thought and Culture*, Cambridge: Cambridge University Press.

Westerhoff, J. (2009). *Nāgārjuna's Madhyamaka: A Philosophical Introduction*, Oxford: Oxford University Press.

Wilhelm, H. & Wilhelm, R. (1979). *Understanding the I Ching: The Wilhelm Lectures on the Book of Changes*, Princeton, NJ: Princeton University Press.

Wilhelm, R. & Baynes, C. F., trans. (1977). *The I Ching: Book of Changes*, Princeton, NJ: Princeton University Press.

Williams, P. (1989). *Mahāyāna Buddhism: The Doctrinal Foundations*, London: Routledge.

Zhao, X. (2022). A Buddhist Reconfiguration of John Hick's Pluralistic Hypothesis: A Madhyamaka Perspective. *Religious Studies*, 58(1): 180–96. https://doi.org/10.1017/S0034412520000256.

Ziporyn, B., ed. and trans. (2009). *Zhuangzi: The Essential Writings*, Indianapolis, IN: Hackett.

Acknowledgements

I am grateful to my graduate students at the University of Macau for bringing the ideas presented here to life through many animated discussions. I have a particular debt of gratitude to John Zhao for his enthusiasm for the project and his insight. I am also indebted to my colleague and friend Damian Shaw for his astute observations and grammatical prowess. Thanks are also due to an anonymous reviewer for taking the trouble to provide some very helpful feedback on the manuscript. My greatest debt is to my husband, Rhett Gayle, without whom nothing would be possible. This Element is dedicated to my friend and companion 何南南, whose heritage harmonizes East and West.

Cambridge Elements

Philosophy of Religion

Yujin Nagasawa
University of Birmingham

Yujin Nagasawa is Professor of Philosophy and Co-director of the John Hick Centre for Philosophy of Religion at the University of Birmingham. He is currently President of the British Society for the Philosophy of Religion. He is a member of the Editorial Board of *Religious Studies*, the *International Journal for Philosophy of Religion*, and *Philosophy Compass*.

About the Series

This Cambridge Elements series provides concise and structured introductions to all the central topics in the philosophy of religion. It offers balanced, comprehensive coverage of multiple perspectives in the philosophy of religion. Contributors to the series are cutting-edge researchers who approach central issues in the philosophy of religion. Each provides a reliable resource for academic readers and develops new ideas and arguments from a unique viewpoint.

Cambridge Elements

Philosophy of Religion

Elements in the Series

Ontological Arguments
Tyron Goldschmidt

Religious Language
Olli-Pekka Vainio

Deprovincializing Science and Religion
Gregory Dawes

Divine Hiddenness
Veronika Weidner

The Axiology of Theism
Klaas J. Kraay

Religious Experience
Amber L. Griffioen

Feminism, Religion and Practical Reason
Beverley Clack

Pantheism
Andrei A. Buckareff

God and Prayer
Scott A. Davison

Death and Persistence
Rebekah L. H. Rice

Eastern Philosophy of Religion
Victoria S. Harrison

A full series listing is available at: www.cambridge.org/EPREL

Printed in the United States
by Baker & Taylor Publisher Services